everyday

tapas

PaRragon

Bath · New York · Singapore · Hong Kong · Cologne · Delhi · Melbourne

This edition published by parragon in 2008

Parragon Publishing
Queen Street House
4 Queen Street
Bath BA1 1HE, UK

ISBN 978-1-4075-3024-6

Printed in China

This book uses imperial, metric, and US cup measurements. Follow the same units of measurement throughout; do not mix imperial and metric. All spoon measurements are level, unless otherwise stated: teaspoons are assumed to be 5ml, and tablespoons are assumed to be 15ml. Unless otherwise stated, milk is assumed to be whole, eggs and individual fruits such as bananas are medium, and pepper is freshly ground black pepper.

Recipes using raw or very lightly cooked eggs should be avoided by infants, the elderly, pregnant women, convalescents, and anyone suffering from an illness. Pregnant and breast-feeding women are advised to avoid eating peanuts and peanut products.

everyday
tapas

introduction

Tapas has become a bit of a buzzword in the last few years, but what exactly is tapas, and where does it come from?

Tapas is the collective name for small, delicious mouthfuls of something savory, served with a chilled white wine, beer, or sherry. It comes from tapa, the Spanish word for lid – specifically, the "lid" created by the slice of bread that an innkeeper would thoughtfully place on top of a customer's wine glass to keep out the flies and dust between sips. The Andalucians then came up with the idea of balancing a morsel of something tasty on top of the bread to nibble on – a few cubes of cheese or ham – and a new Spanish institution

was born. Today, tapas are served in almost every bar throughout Spain. Usually they are displayed on the bar, and the waiter puts your selection on a plate, for eating either standing up or seated at the bar or a table.

Everything about tapas, from the preparation to eating and enjoying it, is a uniquely Spanish experience. Tapas are what eating is all about, a true feast for the senses – they look and smell delectable, and taste even better. Serve them on pretty plates in bright colors to bring a little Spanish sunshine to a cloudy day.

How you use tapas is up to you. A simple selection of these bite-size gastronomic glories can be served with drinks before lunch or dinner, or an array of dishes can make an informal lunch or dinner in themselves. Tapas are made from a wonderful variety of foods – meat, seafood, eggs, nuts, and cheese, as well as every vibrant vegetable imaginable, in healthy Mediterranean style, with

dips and sauces to add even more flavor and interest to the tapas experience.

Eating tapas goes hand-in-hand with hospitality, friendship, and plenty of good conversation, so tuck in, forget the cares of the day, and linger, Spanish-style, with your favorite people.

nibbles

The Spanish have succeeded in elevating pre-lunch or dinner drinks and nibbles to irresistible heights. Succulent green and black olives marinated in herb- and spice-flavored oil, crunchy roasted almonds coated in coarse sea salt and smoky paprika, bite-size tarts and pizzas, sizzling shrimp, chunks of juicy steak or chorizo, dips that taste of pure sunshine, stuffed tomatoes, asparagus spears wrapped in Serrano ham, the must-have ingredient for a Spanish-themed party – the recipes are all here, and all that you need to do is choose what you are going to drink as you tuck in and let your imagination take you to another land.

Toothpicks are an essential tool when it comes to eating tapas, so provide plenty. In some Spanish bars, all the tapas are served on toothpicks, and the number of toothpicks you leave behind determine the size of your bill – but if you are serving tapas at a party, your objective in providing toothpicks is to keep your guests' hands as clean as possible, because eating these tasty morsels can become a very messy business!

If you are planning to serve marinated olives, remember to prepare these ahead of time, because they benefit from being steeped in their flavorings for a day or two, or even longer.

olives with orange & lemon

ingredients

SERVES 4–6

2 tsp. fennel seeds
2 tsp. cumin seeds
8 oz/225 g/1¼ cups
    green olives
8 oz/225 g/1¼ cups
    black olives
2 tsp. grated orange rind
2 tsp. grated lemon rind
3 shallots, finely chopped
pinch of ground cinnamon
4 tbsp. white wine vinegar
5 tbsp. olive oil
2 tbsp. orange juice
1 tbsp. chopped fresh mint
1 tbsp. chopped fresh parsley

method

Dry-fry the fennel seeds and cumin seeds in a small, heavy-bottom skillet, shaking the skillet frequently, until they begin to pop and give off their aroma. Remove the skillet from the heat and let cool.

Place the olives, orange and lemon rind, shallots, cinnamon, and toasted seeds in a bowl.

Whisk the vinegar, olive oil, orange juice, mint, and parsley together in a bowl and pour over the olives. Toss well, then cover and let chill for 1–2 days before serving.

cracked marinated olives

ingredients

SERVES 8

1 lb/450 g can or jar unpitted
    large green olives, drained

4 garlic cloves, peeled

2 tsp. coriander seeds

1 small lemon

4 sprigs of fresh thyme

4 feathery stalks of fennel

2 small fresh red chilies
    (optional)

pepper

Spanish extra-virgin olive oil,
    to cover

method

To allow the flavors of the marinade to penetrate the olives, place on a cutting board and, using a rolling pin, bash them lightly so that they crack slightly. Alternatively, use a sharp knife to cut a lengthwise slit in each olive as far as the pit. Using the flat side of a broad knife, lightly crush each garlic clove. Using a mortar and pestle, crack the coriander seeds. Cut the lemon, with its rind, into small chunks.

Put the olives, garlic, coriander seeds, lemon chunks, thyme sprigs, fennel, and chilies, if using, in a large bowl and toss together. Season with pepper to taste, but you should not need to add salt as preserved olives are usually salty enough. Pack the ingredients tightly into a glass jar with a lid. Pour in enough olive oil to cover the olives, then seal the jar tightly.

Let the olives stand at room temperature for 24 hours, then marinate in the refrigerator for at least 1 week but preferably 2 weeks before serving. From time to time, gently give the jar a shake to remix the ingredients. Return the olives to room temperature and remove from the oil to serve. Provide toothpicks for spearing the olives.

olives wrapped with anchovies

ingredients

MAKES 12

12 anchovy fillets in oil, drained

24 pimiento-stuffed green
olives in oil, drained

method

Using a sharp knife, halve each anchovy fillet lengthwise.
Wrap a half fillet around the middle of each olive, overlapping
the ends, and secure with a wooden toothpick. Repeat with
another olive and anchovy fillet half and slide onto the
toothpick. Continue until all the ingredients are used.
Serve immediately or cover until required.

paprika-spiced almonds

ingredients

MAKES 1 LB 2 OZ/500 G
SERVES 4–6

1 1/2 tbsp. coarse sea salt

1/2 tsp. smoked sweet
Spanish paprika, or hot
paprika, to taste

1 lb 2 oz/500 g blanched
almonds

extra-virgin olive oil

method

Preheat the oven to 400°F/200°C. Place the sea salt and paprika in a mortar and grind with the pestle to a fine powder. Alternatively, use a mini spice blender (the amount is too small to process in a full-size processor).

Place the almonds on a baking sheet and toast in the preheated oven for 8–10 minutes, stirring occasionally, until golden and giving off a toasted aroma. Watch after 7 minutes because they burn quickly. Pour into a heatproof bowl.

Drizzle over 1 tablespoon of olive oil and stir to ensure all the nuts are lightly and evenly coated. Add extra oil, if necessary. Sprinkle with the salt and paprika mixture and stir again. Transfer to a small bowl and serve at room temperature.

salted almonds

ingredients

SERVES 6–8

8 oz/225 g/scant 1½ cups
whole almonds, in their
skins or blanched (see
method)
4 tbsp. Spanish olive oil
coarse sea salt
1 tsp. paprika or ground
cumin (optional)

method

Preheat the oven to 350°F/180°C. Fresh almonds in their skins are superior in taste, but blanched almonds are much more convenient. If the almonds are not blanched, put them in a bowl, cover with boiling water for 3–4 minutes, then plunge them into cold water for 1 minute. Drain them well in a strainer, then slide off the skins between your fingers. Dry the almonds well on paper towels.

Put the olive oil in a roasting pan and swirl it round so that it covers the bottom. Add the almonds and toss them in the pan so that they are evenly coated in the oil, then spread them out in a single layer.

Roast the almonds in the oven for 20 minutes, or until they are light golden brown, tossing several times during the cooking. Drain the almonds on paper towels, then transfer them to a bowl.

While the almonds are still warm, sprinkle with plenty of sea salt and the paprika or cumin, if using, and toss well together to coat. Serve the almonds warm or cold. The almonds are at their best when served freshly cooked, so, if possible, cook them on the day that you plan to eat them. However, they can be stored in an airtight container for up to 3 days.

moorish fava bean dip

ingredients

SERVES 6

1 lb 2 oz/500 g shelled fresh
    or frozen fava beans
5 tbsp. olive oil
1 garlic clove, finely chopped
1 onion, finely chopped
1 tsp. ground cumin
1 tbsp. lemon juice
6 fl oz/175 ml/3/4 cup water
1 tbsp. chopped fresh mint
salt and pepper
paprika, to garnish
raw vegetables, crusty bread
    or breadsticks, to serve

method

If using fresh fava beans, bring a large pan of lightly salted water to a boil. Add the beans, then reduce the heat and simmer, covered, for 7 minutes. Drain well, then refresh under cold running water and drain again. Remove and discard the outer skins. If using frozen beans, let thaw completely, then remove and discard the outer skins.

Heat 1 tablespoon of the olive oil in a skillet. Add the garlic, onion, and cumin and cook over low heat, stirring occasionally, until the onion is softened and translucent. Add the fava beans and cook, stirring frequently, for 5 minutes.

Remove the skillet from the heat and transfer the mixture to a food processor or blender. Add the lemon juice, the remaining olive oil, water, and mint and process to a paste. Season to taste with salt and pepper.

Scrape the paste back into the skillet and heat gently until warm. Transfer to individual serving bowls and dust lightly with paprika. Serve with dippers of your choice.

eggplant &
bell pepper dip

ingredients

SERVES 6–8

2 large eggplants

2 red bell peppers

4 tbsp. Spanish olive oil

2 garlic cloves, coarsely
    chopped

grated rind and juice of
    1/2 lemon

1 tbsp. chopped cilantro, plus
    extra sprigs to garnish

1/2–1 tsp. paprika

salt and pepper

bread or toast, to serve

method

Preheat the oven to 375°F/190°C. Prick the skins of the
eggplants and bell peppers all over with a fork and
brush with 1 tablespoon of the olive oil. Place on a
baking sheet and bake for 45 minutes, or until the skins
are beginning to turn black, the flesh of the eggplant is
very soft, and the bell peppers are deflated.

Place the cooked vegetables in a bowl and cover tightly
with a clean, damp dish towel. Alternatively, place the
vegetables in a plastic bag and let stand for about
15 minutes, or until cool enough to handle.

When the vegetables have cooled, cut the eggplants in
half lengthwise, carefully scoop out the flesh and
discard the skin. Cut the eggplant flesh into large
chunks. Remove and discard the stem, core, and seeds
from the bell peppers and cut the flesh into large pieces.

Heat the remaining olive oil in a skillet. Add the eggplant
and bell pepper and cook for 5 minutes. Add the garlic
and cook for 30 seconds.

Turn the contents of the skillet onto paper towels to drain,
then transfer to a food processor. Add the lemon rind and
juice, the chopped cilantro, the paprika, and salt and
pepper to taste, then process until a speckled purée is
formed. Transfer the eggplant and bell pepper dip to a
serving bowl. Serve warm, at room temperature, or let cool
for 30 minutes, then let chill in the refrigerator for at least
1 hour, then serve cold. Garnish with cilantro sprigs and
accompany with thick slices of bread or toast for dipping.

eggplant dip

ingredients

SERVES 6–8

1 large eggplant, about
    14 oz/400 g
5 tbsp. olive oil
2 scallions, finely chopped
1 large garlic clove, crushed
2 tbsp. finely chopped fresh
    parsley
salt and pepper
smoked sweet Spanish
    paprika, to garnish
french bread, to serve

method

Cut the eggplant into thick slices and sprinkle with salt
to draw out any bitterness. Let stand for 30 minutes, then
rinse and pat dry.

Heat 4 tablespoons of the olive oil in a large skillet over
medium–high heat. Add the eggplant slices and cook on
both sides until soft and beginning to brown. Remove from
the skillet and let cool. The slices will release the oil again
as they cool.

Heat the remaining olive oil in the skillet. Add the scallions
and garlic and cook for 3 minutes, or until the scallions
become soft. Remove from the heat and reserve with the
eggplant slices to cool.

Transfer all the ingredients to a food processor and process
just until a coarse purée forms. Transfer to a serving bowl
and stir in the parsley. Taste and adjust the seasoning, if
necessary. Serve immediately, or cover and let chill until
15 minutes before required. Sprinkle with paprika and
serve with French bread.

potato wedges with roasted garlic dip

ingredients

SERVES 8

3 lb/1.3 kg potatoes,
    unpeeled and halved

2 tbsp. olive oil

1 garlic clove, finely chopped

2 tsp. salt

roasted garlic dip

2 garlic bulbs, separated
    into cloves

1 tbsp. olive oil

5 tbsp. sour cream or
    strained plain yogurt

4 tbsp. mayonnaise

paprika, to taste

salt

method

First, make the roasted garlic dip. Preheat the oven to 400°F/ 200°C. Place the garlic cloves in an ovenproof dish, then pour in the olive oil and toss to coat. Spread out in a single layer and roast in the preheated oven for 25 minutes, or until tender. Remove from the oven and let stand until cool enough to handle.

Peel the garlic cloves, then place on a heavy cutting board and sprinkle with a little salt. Mash well with a fork until smooth. Scrape into a bowl and stir in the sour cream and mayonnaise. Season to taste with salt and paprika. Cover the bowl with plastic wrap and let chill until ready to serve.

To cook the potatoes, cut each potato half into 3 wedges and place in a large bowl. Add the olive oil, garlic, and salt and toss well. Transfer the wedges to a roasting pan, then arrange in a single layer and roast in the preheated oven for 1–1$\frac{1}{4}$ hours, or until crisp and golden.

Remove from the oven and transfer to serving bowls. Serve immediately, handing round the roasted garlic dip separately.

zucchini fritters with a dipping sauce

ingredients

SERVES 8

1 lb/450 g baby zucchini

3 tbsp. all-purpose flour

1 tsp. paprika

1 large egg

2 tbsp. milk

corn oil, for pan-frying

coarse sea salt

dipping sauce such as aïoli
(see page 70), fiery tomato
salsa (see page 226) or the
pine nut sauce (see below)

pine nut sauce

3 1/2 oz/100 g/generous
1/2 cup pine nuts

1 garlic clove, peeled

3 tbsp. Spanish extra-virgin
olive oil

1 tbsp. lemon juice

3 tbsp. water

1 tbsp. chopped fresh
flat-leaf parsley

salt and pepper

method

If you have chosen to serve the pine nut sauce with the
zucchini fritters, then make this first. Put the pine nuts
and garlic in a food processor and blend to form a
purée. With the motor still running, gradually add the
olive oil, lemon juice, and water to form a smooth sauce.
Stir in the parsley and season to taste with salt and
pepper. Turn into a serving bowl.

To prepare the zucchini, cut them on the diagonal into
thin slices about 1/4 inch/5 mm thick. Put the flour and
paprika in a plastic bag and mix together. Beat the egg
and milk together in a large bowl.

Add the zucchini slices to the flour mixture and toss well
together until coated. Shake off the excess flour. Pour
enough corn oil into a large, heavy-bottom skillet for a
depth of about 1/2 inch/1 cm, and heat. Dip the zucchini
slices, one at a time, into the egg mixture, then slip
them into the hot oil. Cook the zucchini slices, in
batches of a single layer so that they do not overcrowd
the skillet, for 2 minutes, or until crisp and golden brown.

Using a slotted spoon, remove the zucchini fritters from
the skillet and drain on paper towels. Continue until all
the zucchini slices have been cooked.

Serve the zucchini fritters piping hot, lightly sprinkled
with sea salt. Accompany with a bowl of your chosen
dipping sauce.

bandilleras

ingredients

SERVES 8–10

1 tbsp. white wine vinegar

4 garlic cloves, finely chopped

1 fresh red chili, deseeded
    and finely chopped

1 tbsp. sweet paprika

4 tbsp. olive oil

3 skinless, boneless chicken
    breasts, cut into
    1-inch/2.5-cm cubes

1 avocado

3 tbsp. lemon juice

4 oz/115 g San Simon or
    other smoked cheese,
    diced

8–10 black olives, pitted

8–10 cherry tomatoes

3 oz/85 g Manchego or
    Cheddar cheese, cubed

8–10 pimiento-stuffed green
    olives

½ cantaloupe melon,
    deseeded

5–6 slices serrano ham

picada

4 garlic cloves, finely chopped

6 tbsp. chopped fresh parsley

6 tbsp. pickled cucumber,
    finely chopped

5 fl oz/150 ml/⅔ cup olive oil

method

Mix the vinegar, garlic, chili, paprika, and olive oil together
in a bowl. Add the chicken and stir well to coat, then cover
and let marinate in the refrigerator for at least 2 hours or
preferably overnight.

Heat a large, heavy-bottom skillet. Tip the chicken mixture
into the pan and cook over low heat, stirring frequently,
for 10–15 minutes, or until cooked through. Remove from
the heat and let cool to room temperature, then spear the
chicken pieces with wooden toothpicks.

Peel and stone the avocado and cut into bite-size cubes.
Toss in the lemon juice, then thread onto wooden toothpicks
with the smoked cheese. Thread the black olives, tomatoes,
Manchego cheese, and stuffed olives onto wooden toothpicks.

Scoop out 20 balls from the melon with a melon baller
or teaspoon. Cut the ham into 20 strips and wrap around
the melon balls. Thread the melon balls in pairs onto
wooden toothpicks.

To make the Picada, mix all the ingredients together in a
bowl until thoroughly combined into a fairly thick paste.
Arrange all the filled toothpicks—bandilleras—on a large
serving platter and serve with bowls of Picada.

roasted asparagus
with serrano ham

ingredients

MAKES 12

2 tbsp. Spanish olive oil

6 slices serrano ham

12 asparagus spears

pepper

aïoli (see page 70), to serve

method

Preheat the oven to 400°F/200°C. Place half the olive oil in a roasting pan that will hold the asparagus spears in a single layer and swirl it around so that it covers the base. Cut each slice of serrano ham in half lengthwise.

Trim and discard the coarse woody ends of the asparagus spears, then wrap a slice of ham around the stem end of each spear. Place the wrapped spears in the prepared roasting pan and lightly brush with the remaining olive oil. Season the asparagus with pepper.

Roast the asparagus spears in the preheated oven for 10 minutes, depending on the thickness of the asparagus, until tender but still firm. Do not overcook the asparagus spears, as it is important that they are still firm, so that you can pick them up with your fingers.

Serve the roasted asparagus piping hot, accompanied by a bowl of aïoli for dipping.

ham-wrapped potatoes

ingredients

SERVES 4

12 new potatoes, unpeeled
2 tbsp. olive oil
12 slices serrano ham
salt

method

Preheat the oven to 400°F/200°C. Place the potatoes in a steamer set over a pan of boiling water. Cover and steam for 30 minutes, or until tender. Remove from the heat and let cool slightly.

Pour the olive oil into an ovenproof dish. Wrap each potato in a slice of ham and arrange in the dish in a single layer. Roast in the preheated oven, turning occasionally, for 20 minutes.

Transfer the potatoes to warmed serving dishes. Season to taste with salt and serve immediately or let cool a little before serving.

spicy chicken livers

ingredients

SERVES 4–6

4 oz/115 g/generous ³/₄ cup
    all-purpose flour
¹/₂ tsp. ground cumin
¹/₂ tsp. ground cilantro
¹/₂ tsp. paprika
¹/₄ tsp. freshly grated nutmeg
12 oz/350 g chicken livers
6 tbsp. olive oil
salt and pepper
fresh mint sprigs, to garnish

method

Sift the flour onto a large, shallow plate and stir in the cumin, cilantro, paprika, and nutmeg. Season to taste with salt and pepper.

Trim the chicken livers and pat dry with paper towels. Cut the livers in halves or fourths. Toss in the seasoned flour, a few pieces at a time, shaking off any excess.

Heat the olive oil in a large, heavy-bottom skillet. Cook the livers, in batches, over high heat, stirring frequently, for 3–5 minutes, or until crisp on the outside but still tender in the center. Serve impaled on wooden toothpicks and garnished with mint sprigs.

chicken wings with tomato dressing

ingredients

SERVES 6

6 fl oz/175 ml/3/4 cup olive oil

3 garlic cloves, finely
chopped

1 tsp ground cumin

1 lb 4 oz/1 kg chicken wings

2 tomatoes, peeled,
deseeded, and diced

5 tbsp white wine vinegar

1 tbsp shredded fresh basil
leaves

method

Preheat the oven to 180°C/350°F. Mix 1 tablespoon of
the oil, the garlic, and cumin together in a shallow dish.
Cut off and discard the tips of the chicken wings and
add the wings to the spice mixture, turning to coat.
Cover with plastic wrap and leave to marinate in a cool
place for 15 minutes.

Heat 3 tablespoons of the remaining oil in a large,
heavy-bottom skillet. Add the chicken wings, in batches,
and cook, turning frequently, until golden brown.
Transfer to a roasting tin.

Roast the chicken wings for 10–15 minutes, or until
tender and the juices run clear when the point of a
sharp knife is inserted into the thickest part of the meat.

Meanwhile, mix the remaining olive oil, the tomatoes,
vinegar, and basil together in a bowl.

Using tongs, transfer the chicken wings to a nonmetallic dish. Pour the dressing over them, turning to
coat. Cover with plastic wrap, leave to cool, then chill for
4 hours. Remove from the refrigerator 30–60 minutes
before serving to return them to room temperature.

garlic pan-fried bread & chorizo

ingredients

SERVES 6–8

7 oz/200 g chorizo sausage,
    outer casing removed
4 thick slices 2-day-old
    country bread
Spanish olive oil, for pan-frying
3 garlic cloves, finely
    chopped
2 tbsp. chopped fresh
    flat-leaf parsley
paprika, to garnish

method

Cut the chorizo sausage into $1/2$-inch/1-cm thick slices
and cut the bread, with its crusts still on, into $1/2$-inch/1-cm
cubes. Add enough olive oil to a large, heavy-bottom
skillet so that it generously covers the bottom. Heat the
oil, add the garlic, and cook for 30 seconds–1 minute,
or until lightly browned.

Add the bread cubes to the skillet and pan-fry, stirring
all the time, until golden brown and crisp. Add the
chorizo slices and pan-fry for 1–2 minutes, or until hot.
Using a slotted spoon, remove the bread cubes and
chorizo from the skillet and drain well on paper towels.

Turn the pan-fried bread and chorizo into a warmed
serving bowl, add the chopped parsley, and toss together.
Garnish the dish with a sprinkling of paprika and serve
warm. Accompany with toothpicks so that a piece of
sausage and a cube of bread can be speared together
for eating.

steak bites
with chili sauce

ingredients

SERVES 4–6

2 tbsp. olive oil

1 onion, chopped

1 tsp. paprika

1 garlic clove, finely chopped

1 fresh red chili, seeded
    and sliced

14 oz/400 g canned chopped
    tomatoes

2 tbsp. dry white wine

1 tbsp. tomato paste

1 tbsp. sherry vinegar

2 tsp. sugar

2 rump steaks, about
    6–8 oz/175–225 g each

2 tsp. tabasco sauce

1 tbsp. chopped fresh parsley

salt and pepper

method

Heat half the olive oil in a heavy-bottom saucepan.
Add the onion and cook over low heat, stirring
occasionally, for 5 minutes, or until softened. Add the
paprika, garlic, and chili and cook for an additional
2–3 minutes, then stir in the tomatoes with their juices,
wine, tomato paste, vinegar, and sugar. Simmer gently
for 15–20 minutes, or until thickened.

Meanwhile, heat a heavy-bottom skillet or grill pan over
high heat and brush with the remaining olive oil. Season
the steaks to taste with pepper and rub with the Tabasco,
then add to the pan. Cook for 1–1^1/$_2$ minutes on each
side, or until browned. Reduce the heat and cook, turning
once, for 3 minutes for rare, 4–5 minutes for medium,
or 5–7 minutes for well done. Remove from the heat and
keep warm.

Transfer the sauce to a food processor or blender
and process until fairly smooth. Transfer to a serving
bowl, then season to taste with salt and pepper and stir
in the parsley.

Transfer the steaks to a cutting board and cut into bite-
size pieces. Impale on wooden toothpicks, then place on
serving plates and serve immediately with the sauce.

sizzling chili shrimp

ingredients

SERVES 8

1 lb 2 oz/500 g raw jumbo
    shrimp, in their shells
1 small fresh red chili
6 tbsp. Spanish olive oil
2 garlic cloves, finely
    chopped
pinch of paprika
salt
crusty bread, to serve

method

To prepare the shrimp, pull off their heads. With your fingers, peel off their shells, leaving the tails intact. Using a sharp knife, make a shallow slit along the underside of each shrimp, then pull out the dark vein and discard. Rinse the shrimp under cold water and dry well on paper towels.

Cut the chili in half lengthwise, remove the seeds, and finely chop the flesh. It is important either to wear gloves or to wash your hands very thoroughly after chopping chilies because their juices can cause irritation to sensitive skin, especially round the eyes, nose, or mouth. Whatever you do, don't rub your eyes after touching the cut flesh of the chili.

Heat the olive oil in a large, heavy-bottom skillet or ovenproof casserole until quite hot, then add the garlic and cook for 30 seconds. Add the shrimp, chili, paprika, and a pinch of salt and cook for 2–3 minutes, stirring all the time, until the shrimp turn pink and start to curl.

Serve the shrimp in the cooking dish, still sizzling. Accompany with toothpicks, to spear the shrimp, and chunks or slices of crusty bread to mop up the aromatic cooking oil.

spicy shrimp in sherry

ingredients

SERVES 4

12 raw Mediterranean shrimp
2 tbsp. olive oil
2 tbsp. dry sherry
pinch of cayenne pepper or
    dash of Tabasco sauce
salt and pepper

method

Pull the heads off the shrimp and peel, leaving the tails intact. Cut along the length of the back of each shrimp and remove and discard the dark vein. Rinse and pat dry.

Heat the olive oil in a large, heavy-bottom skillet. Add the shrimp and cook over medium heat, stirring occasionally, for 2–3 minutes, or until they have turned pink. Add the sherry and season to taste with cayenne, salt, and pepper.

Tip the contents of the skillet onto a serving platter. Impale each shrimp with a wooden toothpick and serve.

crab tartlets

ingredients

MAKES 24

1 tbsp. Spanish olive oil

1 small onion, finely chopped

1 garlic clove, finely chopped

splash of dry white wine

2 eggs

5 fl oz/150 ml/²/₃ cup milk or
 light cream

6 oz/175 g canned crabmeat,
 drained

2 oz/55 g/¹/₂ cup manchego
 or Parmesan cheese,
 grated

2 tbsp. chopped fresh
 flat-leaf parsley

pinch of freshly grated nutmeg

salt and pepper

sprigs of fresh dill, to garnish

pie dough

12 oz/150 g/2¹/₄ cups
 all-purpose flour, plus
 extra for dusting

pinch of salt

6 oz/175 g butter

2 tbsp. cold water

or

1 lb 2 oz/500 g ready-made
 unsweetened pastry

method

Preheat the oven to 375°F/190°C. To prepare the crabmeat filling, heat the olive oil in a heavy-bottom skillet, add the onion and cook for 5 minutes, or until softened but not browned. Add the garlic and cook for an additional 30 seconds. Add a splash of wine and cook for 1–2 minutes, or until most of the wine has evaporated.

Lightly whisk the eggs in a large mixing bowl, then whisk in the milk or cream. Add the crabmeat, cheese, and parsley, and the onion mixture. Season the mixture with nutmeg and salt and pepper to taste and mix well together.

To prepare the pie dough if you are making it yourself, mix the flour and salt together in a large mixing bowl. Add the butter, cut into small pieces, and rub in until the mixture resembles fine bread crumbs. Gradually stir in enough of the water to form a firm dough. Alternatively, the pie dough could be made in a food processor.

On a lightly floured counter, thinly roll out the dough. Using a plain, round 2³/₄-inch/7-cm cutter, cut the pastry into 18 circles. Gently pile the trimmings together, roll out again, then cut out an additional 6 circles. Use to line 24 x 1¹/₂-inch/4-cm tartlet pans. Carefully spoon the crabmeat mixture into the pastry shells, taking care not to overfill them. Bake the tartlets in the oven for 25–30 minutes, or until golden brown and set. Serve the crab tartlets hot or cold, garnished with fresh dill sprigs.

spanish spinach & tomato pizzas

ingredients

MAKES 32

2 tbsp. Spanish olive oil, plus
extra for brushing and
drizzling

1 onion, finely chopped

1 garlic clove, finely chopped

14 oz/400 g canned chopped
tomatoes

4½ oz/125 g/scant 3 cups
baby spinach leaves

salt and pepper

2 tbsp. pine nuts

bread dough

4 tbsp. warm water

½ tsp. active dry yeast

pinch of sugar

7 oz/220 g/generous
1¼ cups white bread
flour, plus extra for dusting

½ tsp. salt

method

To make the bread dough, measure the water into a small
bowl, sprinkle in the dry yeast and sugar, and let stand
in a warm place for 10–15 minutes, or until frothy.

Sift the flour and salt into a large bowl. Make a well in the
center, pour in the yeast, then stir together. Work the dough
with your hands until it leaves the sides of the bowl clean,
then turn it out onto a lightly floured counter and knead for
10 minutes, or until smooth and elastic. Put it in a clean
bowl, cover with a clean, damp dish towel and let stand in a
warm place for 1 hour, until risen and doubled in size.

To make the topping, heat the olive oil in a large, heavy-
bottom skillet. Add the onion and cook for 5 minutes, or
until softened but not browned. Add the garlic and cook
for an additional 30 seconds. Stir in the tomatoes and
cook for about 5 minutes, until reduced to a thick mixture.
Add the spinach leaves and cook, stirring, until they
have wilted a little. Season to taste with salt and pepper.

While the dough is rising, preheat the oven to 400°F/200°C.
Brush several baking sheets with olive oil. Turn the dough out
onto a lightly floured counter and knead well for 2–3 minutes
to knock out the air bubbles. Roll out the dough very, very
thinly and, using a 2½-inch/6-cm plain, round cutter, cut out
32 circles. Place on the prepared baking sheets.

Cover each base with the spinach mixture, then sprinkle
the pine nuts on top and drizzle a little olive oil over
each pizza. Bake in the oven for 10–15 minutes, or until
the edges of the dough are golden brown. Serve hot.

stuffed cherry tomatoes

ingredients

SERVES 8

24 cherry tomatoes

anchovy and olive filling
1³/4 oz/50 g canned
    anchovies in olive oil
8 pimiento-stuffed green
    olives, finely chopped
2 large hard-cooked eggs,
    finely chopped
pepper

or

crab salad filling
6 oz/175 g canned crabmeat,
    drained
4 tbsp. mayonnaise
1 tbsp. chopped fresh
    flat-leaf parsley
salt and pepper

or

black olive and caper filling
12 pitted black olives
3 tbsp. capers
6 tbsp. aïoli
salt and pepper

method

Several choices of filling have been given in this recipe,
but to make a selection of each simply cut the filling
quantities to stuff the corresponding number of tomatoes.

If necessary, cut and discard a very thin slice from the
stalk end of each tomato to make the bases flat and stable.
Cut a thin slice from the smooth end of each tomato and
discard. Using a serrated knife or teaspoon, scoop out and
discard the pulp and seeds. Turn the tomatoes upside
down on paper towels and let drain for 5 minutes.

To make the Anchovy and Olive Filling, drain the anchovies,
reserving the oil for later, chop finely, and put in a bowl.
Add the olives and hard-cooked eggs. Pour in a trickle
of oil from the drained anchovies to moisten the mixture,
season with pepper (don't add salt to season as the
anchovies will provide enough) and mix well together.

To make the Crab Salad Filling, put the crabmeat,
mayonnaise, and parsley in a bowl and mix well together.
Season the filling to taste with salt and pepper.

To make the Black Olive and Caper Filling, put the olives
and capers on paper towels to drain them well, then
chop finely and put in a bowl. Add the aïoli and mix well
together. Season the filling to taste with salt and pepper.

Fill a pastry bag fitted with a ³/4-inch/2-cm plain tip with
the filling of your choice and use to pack the filling into
the hollow tomato shells. Store the tomatoes in the
refrigerator until ready to serve.

sauteed garlic mushrooms

ingredients

SERVES 6

1 lb/450 g white mushrooms

5 tbsp. Spanish olive oil

2 garlic cloves, finely
    chopped

squeeze of lemon juice

salt and pepper

4 tbsp. chopped fresh
    flat-leaf parsley

crusty bread, to serve

method

Wipe or brush clean the mushrooms, then trim off the
stalks close to the caps. Cut any large mushrooms in half
or into quarters. Heat the olive oil in a large, heavy-bottom
skillet, add the garlic and cook for 30 seconds–1 minute,
or until lightly browned. Add the mushrooms and sauté
over high heat, stirring most of the time, until the mushrooms
have absorbed all the oil in the skillet.

Reduce the heat to low. When the juices have come out
of the mushrooms, increase the heat again, and sauté
for 4–5 minutes, stirring most of the time, until the juices
have almost evaporated. Add a squeeze of lemon juice
and season to taste with salt and pepper. Stir in the parsley
and cook for an additional minute.

Transfer the sautéed mushrooms to a warmed serving dish
and serve piping hot or warm. Accompany with chunks or
slices of crusty bread for mopping up the garlic cooking juices.

chili mushrooms

ingredients

SERVES 6–8

2 oz/55 g/1/2 stick butter

5 tbsp. olive oil

2 lb 4 oz/1 kg white mushrooms

4 fat garlic cloves, finely
    chopped

1 fresh red chili, deseeded
    and finely chopped

1 tbsp. lemon juice

salt and pepper

fresh parsley sprigs, to garnish

method

Heat the butter with the olive oil in a large, heavy-bottom skillet. When the butter has melted, add the mushrooms, garlic, and chili and cook over medium–low heat, stirring frequently, for 5 minutes.

Stir in the lemon juice and season the mushrooms to taste with salt and pepper.

Transfer to warmed serving dishes and serve immediately, garnished with parsley sprigs.

deep-fried cauliflower

ingredients

SERVES 4–6

1 cauliflower, cut into florets

1 egg

5 fl oz/150 ml/²/₃ cup milk

4 oz/115 g/generous ³/₄ cup
all-purpose flour

vegetable oil, for deep-frying

salt

tomato & bell pepper salsa
(see below), or aïoli (see
page 70), to serve

for the salsa

4 tbsp. olive oil

10 large garlic cloves

5 oz/140 g shallots, chopped

4 large red bell peppers,
deseeded and chopped

2 lb 4 oz/1 kg ripe, fresh
tomatoes, chopped

2 thin strips freshly pared
orange rind

pinch of hot red pepper
flakes, to taste (optional)

salt and pepper

method

To make the salsa, heat the olive oil in a large,
flameproof casserole over a medium heat. Add the garlic,
shallots, and bell peppers and cook for 10 minutes,
stirring occasionally, until the bell peppers are soft, but
not brown. Add the tomatoes, orange rind, hot pepper
flakes, if using, and salt and pepper to taste and bring to
a boil. Reduce the heat to as low as possible and let
simmer, uncovered, for 45 minutes, or until the liquid
evaporates and the sauce thickens. Purée the sauce in
a food processor then press through a fine strainer.

To cook the cauliflower, bring a large pan of lightly salted
water to a boil. Add the cauliflower florets, then reduce
the heat and simmer gently for 5 minutes. Drain well, then
refresh under cold running water and drain again.

Beat the egg and milk together in a bowl until combined.
Gradually whisk in the flour and 1 teaspoon salt.

Meanwhile, heat the vegetable oil for deep-frying to
350–375°F/180–190°C, or until a cube of bread browns
in 30 seconds.

Dip the cauliflower florets in the batter and drain off the
excess, then deep-fry, in batches if necessary, for 5 minutes,
or until golden. Drain on paper towels, then serve immediately
in warmed bowls with tomato & bell pepper salsa or aïoli.

made with vegetables

Many tapas dishes are based on vegetables, which in Spain are treated with great respect and loving care. The Spanish serve tapas vegetable dishes when the vegetables are in season and, for authenticity, you should do the same where possible. However, some of the recipes in this chapter do "cheat" and use vegetables preserved in oil, such as pimientos and artichoke hearts, which are readily available and quite excellent, as well as time-saving.

Potato dishes are particularly popular tapas, and those using baby new potatoes are a great way to take advantage of when these are in season locally. They go very well with aïoli, a rich, garlic mayonnaise from Catalonia. It is well worth acquiring the art of making this delectable sauce from scratch, because it is a tapas classic and appears on every tapas menu. Potato-based tapas dishes can be served as bite-size nibbles on toothpicks, or as side dishes along with some of the other tasty recipes in this chapter that use everything from colorful bell peppers, eggplants, and tomatoes – all of which are very good roasted – to green beans and fava beans, served in a dressing. Other vegetable dishes are made substantial by the addition of a stuffing – rice is particularly suitable for this. Eating vegetables has never looked so good!

roasted bell pepper salad

ingredients

SERVES 8

3 red bell peppers

3 yellow bell peppers

5 tbsp. Spanish extra-virgin
　　olive oil

2 tbsp. dry sherry vinegar or
　　lemon juice

2 garlic cloves, crushed

pinch of sugar

salt and pepper

1 tbsp. capers

8 small black Spanish olives

2 tbsp. chopped fresh
　　marjoram, plus extra
　　sprigs to garnish

method

Preheat the broiler to high. Place the bell peppers on a wire rack or broiler pan and cook under the broiler for 10 minutes, until their skins have blackened and blistered, turning them frequently.

Remove the roasted bell peppers from the heat, and either put them in a bowl and immediately cover tightly with a clean, damp dish towel, or put them in a plastic bag. The steam helps to soften the skins and makes it easier to remove them. Let the peppers stand for about 15 minutes, until they are cool enough to handle.

Holding one bell pepper at a time over a clean bowl, use a sharp knife to make a small hole in the base and gently squeeze out the juices and reserve them. Still holding the bell pepper over the bowl, carefully peel off the blackened skin with your fingers or a knife and discard it. Cut the bell peppers in half and remove the stem, core, and seeds, then cut each bell pepper into neat thin strips. Arrange the bell pepper strips attractively on a serving dish.

To the reserved pepper juices add the olive oil, sherry vinegar, garlic, sugar, and salt and pepper to taste. Whisk together until combined. Drizzle the dressing evenly over the salad.

Sprinkle the capers, olives, and chopped marjoram over the salad, garnish with marjoram sprigs, and serve at room temperature.

red bell peppers with vinegar & capers

ingredients

SERVES 6

1 tbsp. capers

4 tbsp. olive oil

2 lb 4 oz/1 kg red bell
    peppers, halved,
    deseeded and cut
    into strips

4 garlic cloves, finely
    chopped

2 tbsp. sherry vinegar

salt and pepper

method

If using salted capers, brush off most of the salt with your fingers. If using pickled capers in vinegar, drain well and rinse thoroughly.

Heat the oil in a heavy-bottom skillet. Add the bell pepper strips and cook over medium heat, stirring frequently, for 10 minutes, or until softened and charred around the edges. Add the capers and garlic and cook for an additional 2–3 minutes.

Stir in the vinegar and season to taste with salt and pepper—season sparingly with salt if using salted capers. Cook for 1–2 minutes, then remove from the heat. Serve immediately or let cool. Cover and chill before serving.

roasted bell peppers with honey & almonds

ingredients

SERVES 6

8 red bell peppers, cut into
    fourths and deseeded
4 tbsp. olive oil
2 garlic cloves, thinly sliced
1 oz/25 g flaked almonds
2 tbsp. clear honey
2 tbsp. sherry vinegar
2 tbsp. chopped fresh parsley
salt and pepper

method

Preheat the broiler to high. Place the bell peppers, skin-side up, in a single layer on a baking sheet. Cook under the hot broiler for 8–10 minutes, or until the skins have blistered and blackened. Using tongs, transfer to a plastic bag. Tie the top and let cool.

When the bell peppers are cool enough to handle, peel off the skin with your fingers or a knife and discard it. Chop the flesh into bite-size pieces and place in a bowl.

Heat the olive oil in a large, heavy-bottom skillet. Add the garlic and cook over low heat, stirring frequently, for 4 minutes, or until golden. Stir in the almonds, honey, and vinegar, then pour the mixture over the bell pepper pieces. Add the parsley and season to taste with salt and pepper, then toss well.

Let cool to room temperature before transferring to serving dishes. The bell peppers may also be covered and stored in the refrigerator, but should be returned to room temperature to serve.

stuffed pimientos

ingredients

SERVES 7–8

61/2 oz/185 g bottled whole
   pimientos del piquillo

fillings
curd cheese and herb

8 oz/225 g/1 cup curd cheese
1 tsp. lemon juice
1 garlic clove, crushed
4 tbsp. chopped fresh
   flat-leaf parsley
1 tbsp. chopped fresh mint
1 tbsp. chopped fresh
   oregano
salt and pepper

tuna mayonnaise

7 oz/200 g canned tuna steak
   in olive oil, drained
5 tbsp. mayonnaise
2 tsp. lemon juice
2 tbsp. chopped fresh
   flat-leaf parsley
salt and pepper

goat cheese and olive

13/4 oz/50 g pitted black
   olives, finely chopped
7 oz/200 g soft goat cheese
1 garlic clove, crushed
salt and pepper

method

There is a choice of fillings provided in this recipe—the final decision is yours. Lift the peppers from the jar, reserving the oil for later.

To make the Curd Cheese and Herb Filling, put the curd cheese in a bowl and add the lemon juice, garlic, parsley, mint, and oregano. Mix well together. Season to taste with salt and pepper.

To make the Tuna and Mayonnaise Filling, put the tuna in a bowl and add the mayonnaise, lemon juice, and parsley. Add 1 tablespoon of the reserved oil from the jar of pimientos and mix well. Season to taste with salt and pepper.

To make the Goat Cheese and Olive Filling, put the olives in a bowl, and add the goat cheese, garlic, and 1 tablespoon of the reserved oil from the jar of pimientos. Mix well together. Season to taste with salt and pepper.

Using a teaspoon, heap the filling of your choice into each pimiento. Put in the refrigerator and let chill for at least 2 hours until firm.

To serve the pimientos, arrange them on a serving plate and, if necessary, wipe with paper towels to remove any of the filling that has spread over the skins.

stuffed bell peppers

ingredients

MAKES 6

6 tbsp. olive oil, plus a little
   extra for rubbing on
   bell peppers
2 onions, finely chopped
2 garlic cloves, crushed
5 oz/140 g/^{2}/$_3$ cup Spanish
   short-grain rice
2 oz/55 g/^{1}/$_3$ cup raisins
2 oz/55 g/^{1}/$_3$ cup pine nuts
1^1/$_2$ oz/40 g/generous ^{1}/$_2$ cup
   fresh parsley, finely
   chopped
1 tbsp. tomato paste dissolved
   in 3 cups hot water
salt and pepper
4–6 red, green, or yellow bell
   peppers (or a mix of colors),
   or 6 of the long,
   mediterranean variety

method

Preheat the oven to 400°F/200°C. Heat the oil in a shallow,
heavy-bottom flameproof casserole. Add the onions and
cook for 3 minutes. Add the garlic and cook for an additional
2 minutes, or until the onion is soft but not brown.

Stir in the rice, raisins, and pine nuts until all are coated
in the oil, then add half the parsley and salt and pepper
to taste. Stir in the tomato paste and bring to a boil. Reduce
the heat and let simmer, uncovered, shaking the casserole
frequently, for 20 minutes, or until the rice is tender, the
liquid is absorbed and small holes appear on the surface.
Watch carefully because the raisins can catch and burn.
Stir in the remaining parsley, then let cool slightly.

While the rice is simmering, cut the top off each bell
pepper and reserve. Remove the core and seeds from
each bell pepper.

Divide the stuffing equally between the bell peppers. Use
wooden toothpicks to secure the tops back in place. Lightly
rub each bell pepper with olive oil and arrange in a single
layer in a baking dish. Bake in the preheated oven for
30 minutes, or until the bell peppers are tender. Serve
hot or let cool to room temperature.

baby potatoes
with aïoli

ingredients

SERVES 6–8

1 lb/450 g baby new potatoes

1 tbsp. chopped fresh
    flat-leaf parsley

salt

for the aïoli

1 large egg yolk, at room
    temperature

1 tbsp. white wine vinegar or
    lemon juice

2 large garlic cloves, peeled

salt and pepper

5 tbsp. Spanish extra-virgin
    olive oil

5 tbsp. corn oil

method

To make the aïoli, put the egg yolk, vinegar, garlic, and salt and pepper to taste in the bowl of a food processor fitted with the metal blade and blend well together. With the motor still running, very slowly add the olive oil, then the corn oil, drop by drop at first, then, when it starts to thicken, in a slow, steady stream until the sauce is thick and smooth. Alternatively, mix in a bowl with a whisk.

For this recipe, the aïoli should be a little thin so that it coats the potatoes. To ensure this, quickly blend in 1 tablespoon water so that it forms the consistency of sauce.

To prepare the potatoes, cut them in half or fourths to make bite-size pieces. If they are very small, you can leave them whole. Put the potatoes in a large pan of cold, salted water and bring to a boil. Lower the heat and let simmer for 7 minutes, or until just tender. Drain well, then turn out into a large bowl.

While the potatoes are still warm, pour over the aïoli sauce, and gently toss the potatoes in it. Adding the sauce to the potatoes while they are still warm will help them to absorb the garlic flavor. Let stand for about 20 minutes to allow the potatoes to marinate in the sauce.

Transfer the potatoes with aïoli to a warmed serving dish, sprinkle over the parsley and salt to taste, and serve warm. Alternatively, the aïoli can be served separately, allowing diners to dip the potatoes themselves.

pan-fried potatoes with piquant paprika

ingredients

SERVES 6

3 tsp. paprika

1 tsp. ground cumin

1/4–1/2 tsp. cayenne pepper

1/2 tsp. salt

1 lb/450 g small old potatoes, peeled

corn oil, for pan-frying

sprigs of fresh flat-leaf parsley, to garnish

aïoli, to serve (see page 70) (optional)

method

Put the paprika, cumin, cayenne pepper, and salt in a small bowl and mix well together. Set aside.

Cut each potato into 8 thick wedges. Pour corn oil into a large, heavy-bottom skillet to a depth of about 1 inch/2.5 cm. Heat the oil, then add the potato wedges, preferably in a single layer, and cook gently for 10 minutes, or until golden brown all over, turning from time to time. Remove from the skillet with a slotted spoon and let drain on paper towels.

Transfer the potato wedges to a large bowl and, while they are still hot, sprinkle with the paprika mixture, then gently toss them together to coat.

Turn the potatoes into a large, warmed serving dish, several smaller ones, or individual plates and serve hot, garnished with parsley sprigs. Accompany with a bowl of aïoli for dipping, if wished.

spanish potatoes

ingredients

SERVES 4

2 tbsp. olive oil

1 lb 2 oz/500 g small new
potatoes, halved

1 onion, halved and sliced

1 green bell pepper, deseeded
and cut into strips

1 tsp. chili powder

1 tsp. mustard

10 fl oz/300 ml/1¼ cups
strained tomatoes

10 fl oz/300 ml/1¼ cups
vegetable stock

salt and pepper

chopped fresh parsley,
to garnish

method

Heat the olive oil in a large, heavy-bottom skillet. Add
the new potatoes and sliced onion and cook, stirring
frequently, for 4–5 minutes, or until the onion slices are
soft and translucent.

Add the bell pepper strips, chili powder, and mustard to
the skillet and cook for 2–3 minutes.

Stir the strained tomatoes and vegetable stock into the
skillet and bring to a boil. Reduce the heat and let
simmer for 25 minutes, or until the potatoes are tender.
Season to taste with salt and pepper.

Transfer the potatoes to a warmed serving dish. Sprinkle
the chopped parsley over the top and serve immediately.

Alternatively, let the potatoes cool completely and serve
cold, at room temperature.

feisty potatoes

ingredients

SERVES 6

2 lb 4 oz/1 kg potatoes,
    unpeeled
olive oil
sea salt

chili oil

2/3 cup olive oil
2 small hot fresh red chilies,
    slit
1 tsp. hot Spanish paprika

to serve

aïoli (see page 70)

method

To make the chili oil, heat the olive oil and chilies over high heat until the chilies begin to sizzle. Remove the pan from the heat and stir in the paprika. Set aside and let cool, then transfer the chili oil to a pourer with a spout. Do not strain.

To cook the potatoes, first scrub them, pat them dry, and cut into chunky pieces.

Put 1/2 inch/1 cm olive oil and one potato piece in one or two large, heavy-bottom skillets over medium–high heat and heat until the potato begins to sizzle. Add the remaining potatoes, without crowding the pans, and fry for 15 minutes, or until golden brown all over and tender. Work in batches, if necessary, keeping the cooked potatoes warm while you fry the remainder.

Use a slotted spoon to transfer the potatoes to a plate covered with crumbled paper towels.

While the potatoes cook, make the aïoli.

To serve, divide the potatoes between 6 serving plates and add a serving of aïoli to each. Drizzle with chili oil and serve warm or at room temperature. In Spain these are served with wooden toothpicks.

warm potato salad

ingredients

SERVES 4–6

6 fl oz/175 ml/³/4 cup olive oil
1 lb/450 g waxy potatoes,
    thinly sliced
2 fl oz/50 ml/¹/4 cup white
    wine vinegar
2 garlic cloves, finely
    chopped
salt and pepper

method

Heat ¹/4 cup of the olive oil in a large, heavy-bottom skillet.
Add the potato slices and season to taste with salt, then
cook over low heat, shaking the skillet occasionally, for
10 minutes. Turn the potatoes over and cook for an
additional 5 minutes, or until tender but not browned.

Meanwhile, pour the vinegar into a small pan. Add the
garlic and season to taste with pepper. Bring to a boil,
then stir in the remaining olive oil.

Transfer the potatoes to a bowl and pour over the dressing.
Toss gently and let stand for 15 minutes. Using a slotted
spoon, transfer the potatoes to individual serving dishes
and serve warm.

fava beans with cheese & shrimp

ingredients

SERVES 6

1 lb 2 oz/500 g shelled fresh
    or frozen fava beans
2 fresh thyme sprigs
8 oz/225 g cooked shelled
    shrimp
8 oz/225 g Queso Majorero or
    Gruyère cheese, diced
6 tbsp. olive oil
2 tbsp. lemon juice
1 garlic clove, finely chopped
salt and pepper

method

Bring a large pan of lightly salted water to a boil. Add the fava beans and 1 thyme sprig, then reduce the heat and simmer, covered, for 7 minutes. Drain well and refresh under cold running water, then drain again.

Unless the fava beans are very young, remove and discard the outer skins. Place the beans in a bowl and add the shrimp and cheese.

Chop the remaining thyme sprig. Whisk the olive oil, lemon juice, garlic, and chopped thyme together in a separate bowl and season to taste with salt and pepper.

Pour the dressing over the bean mixture. Toss lightly and serve.

green beans
with pine nuts

ingredients

SERVES 8

2 tbsp. Spanish olive oil

1 3/4 oz/50 g/scant 1/3 cup
    pine nuts

1/2–1 tsp. paprika

1 lb/450 g green beans

1 small onion, finely chopped

1 garlic clove, finely chopped

salt and pepper

juice of 1/2 lemon

method

Heat the oil in a large, heavy-bottom skillet, add the pine nuts and cook for about 1 minute, stirring all the time and shaking the skillet, until light golden brown. Using a slotted spoon, remove the pine nuts from the skillet, drain well on paper towels, then transfer to a bowl. Set aside the oil in the skillet for later. Add the paprika, according to taste, to the pine nuts, stir together until coated, and then set aside.

Trim the green beans and remove any strings if necessary. Put the beans in a pan, pour over boiling water, return to a boil, and cook for 5 minutes, or until tender but still firm. Drain well in a strainer.

Reheat the oil in the skillet, add the onion and cook for 5–10 minutes, or until softened and starting to brown. Add the garlic and cook for an additional 30 seconds.

Add the beans to the skillet and cook for 2–3 minutes, tossing together with the onion until heated through. Season the beans to taste with salt and pepper.

Turn the contents of the skillet into a warmed serving dish, sprinkle over the lemon juice, and toss together. Sprinkle over the golden pine nuts and serve hot.

mixed beans

ingredients

SERVES 4–6

6 oz/175 g shelled fresh or
  frozen fava beans
4 oz/115 g fresh or frozen
  green beans
4 oz/115 g snow peas
1 shallot, finely chopped
6 fresh mint sprigs
4 tbsp. olive oil
1 tbsp. sherry vinegar
1 garlic clove, finely chopped
salt and pepper

method

Bring a large pan of lightly salted water to a boil. Add the
fava beans and reduce the heat, then cover and simmer
for 7 minutes. Remove the beans with a slotted spoon,
then plunge into cold water and drain. Remove and discard
the outer skins.

Meanwhile, return the pan of salted water to a boil. Add
the green beans and return to a boil again. Drain and
refresh under cold running water. Drain well.

Mix the fava beans, green beans, snow peas, and shallot
together in a bowl. Strip the leaves from the mint sprigs,
then reserve half and add the remainder to the bean
mixture. Finely chop the reserved mint.

Whisk the olive oil, vinegar, garlic, and chopped mint
together in a separate bowl and season to taste with salt
and pepper. Pour the dressing over the bean mixture and
toss lightly to coat. Cover with plastic wrap and let chill
until required.

white bean vinaigrette

ingredients

SERVES 4–6

14 oz/400 g canned wax beans
3 celery stalks, chopped
1 gherkin, finely chopped
5 fl oz/150 ml/$^2/_3$ cup olive oil
4 tbsp. white wine vinegar
1 garlic clove, finely chopped
2 tsp. Dijon mustard
1 tbsp. chopped fresh parsley
pinch of sugar
salt and pepper
snipped fresh chives,
    to garnish

method

Drain the beans and rinse well under cold running water, then drain again. Place the beans, celery, and gherkin in a bowl.

Whisk the olive oil, vinegar, garlic, mustard, parsley, and sugar together in a bowl and season to taste with salt and pepper.

Pour the vinaigrette over the bean mixture and toss well. Transfer to a serving dish and sprinkle with the chives, then serve at room temperature or cover and let chill before serving.

garlic tomatoes

ingredients

SERVES 6

8 deep red tomatoes

3 fresh thyme sprigs, plus
extra to garnish

12 garlic cloves, unpeeled

2¹/₂ fl oz/75 ml/generous ¹/₄
cup olive oil

salt and pepper

method

Preheat the oven to 425°F/220°C. Cut the tomatoes in half lengthwise and arrange, cut-side up, in a single layer in a large, ovenproof dish. Tuck the thyme sprigs and garlic cloves between them.

Drizzle the olive oil all over the tomatoes and season to taste with pepper. Bake in the preheated oven for 40–45 minutes, or until the tomatoes are softened and beginning to char slightly around the edges.

Remove and discard the thyme sprigs. Season the tomatoes to taste with salt and pepper. Garnish with the extra thyme sprigs and serve hot or warm. Squeeze the pulp from the garlic over the tomatoes at the table.

baked tomato nests

ingredients

SERVES 4

4 large ripe tomatoes

4 large eggs

4 tbsp. heavy cream

4 tbsp. grated mature Mahon,
    Manchego, or Parmesan
    cheese

salt and pepper

method

Preheat the oven to 350°F/180°C. Cut a slice off the tops of the tomatoes and, using a teaspoon, carefully scoop out the pulp and seeds without piercing the shells. Turn the tomato shells upside down on paper towels and let drain for 15 minutes. Season the insides of the shells with salt and pepper.

Place the tomatoes in an ovenproof dish just large enough to hold them in a single layer. Carefully break 1 egg into each tomato shell, then top with 1 tablespoon of cream and 1 tablespoon of grated cheese.

Bake in the preheated oven for 15–20 minutes, or until the eggs are just set. Serve hot.

stuffed tomatoes with rice

ingredients

SERVES 4–8

5 oz/140 g/³⁄₄ cup long-grain
    rice
5 oz/140 g/generous ³⁄₄ cup
    black olives,
    pitted and chopped
3 tbsp. olive oil
4 beefsteak or other large
    tomatoes, halved
4 tbsp. chopped fresh parsley
salt and pepper

method

Bring a large pan of lightly salted water to a boil. Add the rice, then return to a boil and stir once. Reduce the heat and cook for 10–15 minutes, or until only just tender. Drain well, then rinse under cold running water and drain again. Line a large, shallow dish with paper towels and spread out the rice on top for about 1 hour to dry.

Mix the rice, olives, and olive oil together in a bowl and season well with pepper. You will probably not require any additional salt. Cover with plastic wrap and let stand at room temperature for 8 hours or overnight.

Cut a slice off the tops of the tomatoes and, using a teaspoon, carefully scoop out and discard the seeds without piercing the shells. Scoop out the flesh, then finely chop and add to the rice and olive mixture. Season the insides of the shells to taste with salt, then turn them upside down on paper towels and let drain for 1 hour.

Pat the insides of the tomato shells dry with paper towels, then divide the rice and olive mixture between them. Sprinkle with the parsley and serve.

artichoke hearts & asparagus

ingredients

SERVES 4–6

1 lb/450 g asparagus spears

14 oz/400 g canned artichoke
    hearts, drained and rinsed

2 tbsp. freshly squeezed
    orange juice

1/2 tsp. finely grated orange rind

2 tbsp. walnut oil

1 tsp. Dijon mustard

salad greens, to serve

salt and pepper

method

Trim and discard the coarse, woody ends of the asparagus spears. Make sure all the stems are about the same length, then tie them together loosely with clean kitchen string. If you have an asparagus steamer, you don't need to tie the stems together—just place them in the basket.

Bring a tall pan of lightly salted water to a boil. Add the asparagus, making sure that the tips are protruding above the water, then reduce the heat and let simmer for 10–15 minutes, or until tender. Test by piercing a stem just above the water level with the point of a sharp knife. Drain, then refresh under cold running water and drain again.

Cut the asparagus spears into 1-inch/2.5-cm pieces, keeping the tips intact. Cut the artichoke hearts into small wedges and combine with the asparagus in a bowl.

Whisk the orange juice, orange rind, walnut oil, and mustard together in a bowl and season to taste with salt and pepper. If serving immediately, pour the dressing over the artichoke hearts and asparagus and toss lightly.

Arrange the salad greens in individual serving dishes and top with the artichoke and asparagus mixture. Serve immediately. Alternatively, store the salad, covered, in the refrigerator and add the dressing just before serving.

artichoke hearts & peas

ingredients

SERVES 4–6

4 tbsp. extra-virgin olive oil

2 onions, sliced finely

1 large garlic clove, crushed

10 oz/280 g artichoke hearts
    preserved in oil, drained
    and halved

1 3/4 cups frozen or fresh
    shelled peas

2 red bell peppers, broiled,
    seeded, and sliced

2 thin slices serrano ham,
    chopped (optional),
    or prosciutto

6 tbsp. finely chopped fresh
    parsley

juice 1/2 lemon

salt and pepper

method

Heat the oil in a flameproof casserole over medium-high heat. Add the onions and cook, stirring, for 3 minutes, then add the garlic and cook for 2 minutes until the onions are soft, but not brown.

Add the halved artichoke hearts and fresh peas, if using, along with just enough water to cover. Bring to a boil, then reduce the heat and let simmer for 5 minutes, uncovered, or until the peas are cooked through and all the water has evaporated.

Stir in the bell peppers, ham, and frozen peas, if using. Continue simmering just long enough to warm through. Stir in the parsley and lemon juice to taste. Add salt and pepper, remembering that the ham is salty. Serve at once, or let cool to room temperature.

stuffed mushrooms

ingredients

SERVES 6

6 oz/175 g1¹/2 sticks butter
4 garlic cloves, finely
    chopped
6 large open mushrooms,
    stems removed
2 oz/55 g/1 cup fresh white
    bread crumbs
1 tbsp. chopped fresh thyme
1 egg, lightly beaten
salt and pepper

method

Preheat the oven to 350°F/180°C. Cream the butter in a bowl until softened, then beat in the garlic. Divide two-thirds of the garlic butter between the mushroom caps and arrange them, cup-side up, on a baking sheet.

Melt the remaining garlic butter in a heavy-bottom or nonstick skillet. Add the bread crumbs and cook over low heat, stirring frequently, until golden. Remove from the heat and tip into a bowl. Stir in the thyme and season to taste with salt and pepper. Stir in the beaten egg until thoroughly combined.

Divide the bread-crumb mixture between the mushroom caps and bake in the preheated oven for 15 minutes, or until the stuffing is golden brown and the mushrooms are tender. Serve hot or warm.

marinated eggplants

ingredients

SERVES 4

2 eggplants, halved lengthwise
4 tbsp. olive oil
2 garlic cloves, finely chopped
2 tbsp. chopped fresh parsley
1 tbsp. chopped fresh thyme
2 tbsp. lemon juice
salt and pepper

method

Make 2–3 slashes in the flesh of the eggplant halves and place, cut-side down, in an ovenproof dish. Season to taste with salt and pepper, then pour over the olive oil and sprinkle with the garlic, parsley, and thyme. Cover and let marinate at room temperature for 2–3 hours.

Preheat the oven to 350°F/180°C. Uncover the dish and roast the eggplants in the preheated oven for 45 minutes. Remove the dish from the oven and turn the eggplants over. Baste with the cooking juices and sprinkle with the lemon juice. Return to the oven and cook for an additional 15 minutes.

Transfer the eggplants to serving plates. Spoon over the cooking juices and serve hot or warm.

charbroiled leeks

ingredients

SERVES 4

8 baby leeks
2 tbsp. olive oil, plus extra
    for brushing
2 tbsp. white wine vinegar
2 tbsp. snipped fresh chives
2 tbsp. chopped fresh parsley
1 tsp. Dijon mustard
salt and pepper
fresh parsley sprigs,
    to garnish

method

Trim the leeks and halve lengthwise. Rinse well to remove any grit and pat dry with paper towels.

Heat a grill pan and brush with olive oil. Add the leeks and cook over medium–high heat, turning occasionally, for 5 minutes. Transfer to a shallow dish.

Meanwhile, whisk the olive oil, vinegar, chives, parsley, and mustard together in a bowl and season to taste with salt and pepper. Pour over the leeks, turning to coat. Cover with plastic wrap and let marinate at room temperature, turning occasionally, for 30 minutes.

Divide the leeks between individual serving plates, then garnish with parsley sprigs and serve.

orange & fennel salad

ingredients

SERVES 4

4 large, juicy oranges

1 large fennel bulb, very thinly sliced

1 mild white onion, finely sliced

2 tbsp. extra-virgin olive oil

12 plump black olives, pitted and thinly sliced

1 fresh red chili, deseeded and very thinly sliced (optional)

finely chopped fresh parsley

French bread, to serve

method

Finely grate the rind from the oranges into a bowl and reserve. Using a small, serrated knife, remove all the white pith from the oranges, working over a bowl to catch the juices. Cut the oranges horizontally into thin slices.

Toss the orange slices with the fennel and onion slices. Whisk the olive oil into the reserved orange juice, then spoon over the oranges. Sprinkle the olive slices over the top, add the chili, if using, then sprinkle with the orange rind and parsley. Serve with slices of French bread.

tomato &
olive salad

ingredients

SERVES 6

2 tbsp. sherry or red wine
vinegar

5 tbsp. olive oil

1 garlic clove, finely chopped

1 tsp. paprika

4 tomatoes, peeled and diced

12 anchovy-stuffed or
pimiento-stuffed olives

1/2 cucumber, peeled and
diced

2 shallots, finely chopped

1 tbsp. pickled capers in
brine, drained

2–3 chicory heads, separated
into leaves

salt

method

First, make the dressing. Whisk the vinegar, olive oil, garlic, and paprika together in a bowl. Season to taste with salt and reserve.

Place the tomatoes, olives, cucumber, shallots, and capers in a separate bowl. Pour over the dressing and toss lightly.

Line 6 individual serving bowls with chicory leaves. Spoon an equal quantity of the salad into the center of each and serve.

sweet onion salad

ingredients

SERVES 4–6

4 Spanish onions
2 tbsp. chopped fresh parsley
4 oz/115 g/²/₃ cup black
    olives, pitted
1 tbsp. sherry vinegar
2 tbsp. red wine vinegar
4 fl oz/125 ml/¹/₂ cup olive oil
about 1 tbsp. water
salt and pepper

method

Bring a large pan of lightly salted water to a boil. Add the onions and simmer for 20 minutes, or until tender. Drain and let stand until cool enough to handle.

Thickly slice the onions and place in a shallow dish. Sprinkle over the parsley and olives and season to taste with pepper.

Whisk the vinegars and olive oil together in a bowl, then whisk in enough of the water to make a creamy vinaigrette.

Pour the dressing over the onions and olives and serve at room temperature.

for meat lovers

Although meat has never been as plentiful in Spain as it is in other countries, it does have a place in the culinary repertoire and the recipes in this chapter include the usual pork, lamb, beef, and chicken that are available elsewhere. Of these, pork and chicken are perhaps the most popular with the Spaniards, as are cured Serrano ham and chorizo, the country's favorite sausage, which is flavored with paprika and garlic and can be eaten cold or pan-fried, baked, or cooked in a sauce.

If possible, serve these meat tapas dishes in small, earthenware bowls, just as they are seen on every bar counter in Spain. This is not just for the sake of authenticity, although they certainly look attractive – but also because they retain the heat or cold well, so will keep your tapas dish at the correct temperature while you and your guests relax over a glass of something chilled.

Some of these meat tapas make perfect light lunch or supper dishes – serve them with a salad and some good fresh country bread to mop up the juices. Try serving meatballs this way and you'll have a taste of something delicious to eat and also of a little Spanish history, as meatballs have been a feature of Spanish cookery since as far back as the thirteenth century.

fried chorizo with herbs

ingredients

SERVES 6–8

1 lb 9 oz/700 g chorizo
    cooking sausage
2 tbsp. olive oil
2 garlic cloves, finely
    chopped
4 tbsp. chopped mixed fresh
    herbs

method

Using a sharp knife, cut the chorizo into $1/4$-inch/5-mm thick slices. Heat a large, heavy-bottom skillet. Add the chorizo slices, without any additional fat, and cook over medium heat, stirring frequently, for 5 minutes, or until crisp and browned.

Remove the chorizo slices with a spatula or slotted spoon and drain well on paper towels. Drain the fat from the skillet and wipe out with a pad of paper towels.

Heat the olive oil in the skillet over a medium–low heat. Add the chorizo slices, garlic, and herbs and cook, stirring occasionally, until heated through. Serve immediately.

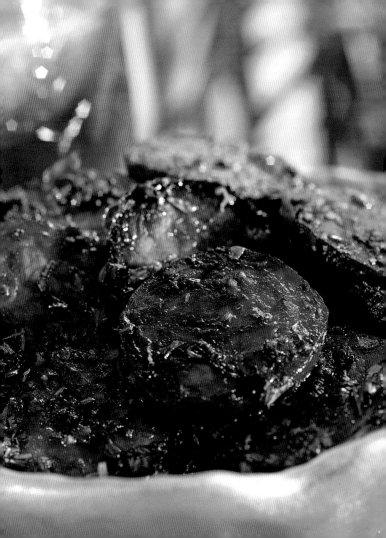

a salad of melon, chorizo & artichokes

ingredients

SERVES 8

12 small globe artichokes

juice of 1/2 lemon

2 tbsp. Spanish olive oil

1 small orange-fleshed
    melon, such as
    cantaloupe

7 oz/200 g chorizo sausage,
    outer casing removed

few sprigs of fresh tarragon or
    flat-leaf parsley, to garnish

dressing

3 tbsp. Spanish extra-virgin
    olive oil

1 tbsp. red wine vinegar

1 tsp. prepared mustard

1 tbsp. chopped fresh
    tarragon

salt and pepper

method

To prepare the artichokes, cut off the stalks. With your hands, break off the toughest outer leaves at the base until the tender inside leaves are visible. Cut the spiky tips off the leaves with a pair of scissors. Using a sharp knife, pare the dark green skin from the base and down the stem. Either brush the cut surfaces of the artichokes with lemon juice as you prepare them to prevent discoloration, or drop them into a bowl of cold water with a little lemon juice added. Unless you are using very young artichokes, carefully remove the choke (the mass of silky hairs) by pulling it out with your fingers or scooping it out with a spoon. It is important to remove all the choke as the little barbs, if eaten, can irritate the throat. Cut the artichokes into fourths and brush them again with lemon juice.

Heat the olive oil in a large, heavy-bottom skillet, then add the artichokes and cook, stirring frequently, for 5 minutes, or until the leaves are golden brown. Transfer the artichokes to a large serving bowl, and let cool.

To prepare the melon, cut in half and scoop out the seeds with a spoon. Cut the flesh into bite-size cubes. Add to the cooled artichokes. Cut the chorizo into bite-size chunks and add to the melon and artichokes.

To make the dressing, put all the ingredients in a small bowl and whisk together. Just before serving, pour the dressing over the salad and toss together. Serve the salad garnished with tarragon or parsley sprigs.

chickpeas & chorizo

ingredients

SERVES 4–6

9 oz/250 g chorizo sausage in
     1 piece, outer casing
     removed

4 tbsp. olive oil

1 onion, finely chopped

1 large garlic clove, crushed

14 oz/400 g canned chickpeas,
     drained and rinsed

6 pimientos del piquillo,
     drained, patted dry,
     and sliced

1 tbsp. sherry vinegar,
     or to taste

salt and pepper

finely chopped fresh parsley,
     to garnish

crusty bread slices, to serve

method

Cut the chorizo into ¹/₂-inch/1-cm dice. Heat the oil in a heavy-bottom skillet over medium heat, then add the onion and garlic. Cook, stirring occasionally, until the onion is softened but not browned. Stir in the chorizo and cook until heated through.

Tip the mixture into a bowl and stir in the chickpeas and pimientos. Splash with sherry vinegar and season to taste with salt and pepper. Serve hot or at room temperature, generously sprinkled with parsley, with plenty of crusty bread.

chorizo empanadillas

ingredients

MAKES 12

4¹/₂ oz/125 g chorizo sausage,
    outer casing removed
all-purpose flour, for dusting
9 oz/250 g ready-made puff
    pastry, thawed if frozen
beaten egg, to glaze
paprika, to garnish

method

Preheat the oven to 400°F/200°C. Cut the chorizo sausage into small dice measuring about ¹/₂ inch/1 cm square.

On a lightly floured counter, thinly roll out the puff pastry. Using a plain, round 3¹/₄-inch/8-cm cutter, cut into circles. Gently pile the trimmings together, roll out again, then cut out additional circles to produce 12 in total. Put about a teaspoonful of the chopped chorizo onto each of the pastry circles.

Dampen the edges of the pastry with a little water, then fold one half over the other half to completely cover the chorizo. Seal the edges together with your fingers. Using the prongs of a fork, press against the edges to give a decorative finish and seal them further. With the tip of a sharp knife, make a small slit in the side of each pastry. You can store the pastries in the refrigerator at this stage until you are ready to bake them.

Place the pastries onto dampened baking sheets and brush each with a little beaten egg to glaze. Bake in the oven for 10–15 minutes, or until golden brown and puffed. Using a small strainer, lightly dust the top of each empanadilla with a little paprika to garnish. Serve the chorizo empanadillas hot or warm.

chorizo &
mushroom kabobs

ingredients

MAKES 25

2 tbsp. olive oil

25 pieces chorizo sausage,
    each about 1/2-inch/1-cm
    square (about 3 1/2 oz/100 g)

25 white mushrooms, wiped
    and stems removed

1 green bell pepper, broiled,
    peeled, and cut into
    5 squares

method

Heat the olive oil in a skillet over medium heat. Add the chorizo and cook for 20 seconds, stirring.

Add the mushrooms and continue cooking for an additional 1–2 minutes until the mushrooms begin to brown and absorb the fat in the skillet.

Thread a bell pepper square, a piece of chorizo, and a mushroom onto a wooden toothpick. Continue until all the ingredients are used. Serve hot or at room temperature.

chorizo in red wine

ingredients

SERVES 6

7 oz/200 g chorizo sausage

7 fl oz/200 ml/generous
    3/4 cup Spanish red wine

2 tbsp. brandy (optional)

fresh flat-leaf parsley sprigs,
    to garnish

crusty bread, to serve

method

Before you begin, bear in mind that this dish is best if prepared the day before you are planning to serve it. Using a fork, prick the chorizo in 3 or 4 places and pour wine over. Place the chorizo and wine in a large pan. Bring the wine to a boil, then reduce the heat and simmer gently, covered, for 15–20 minutes. Transfer the chorizo and wine to a bowl or dish, cover and let the sausage marinate in the wine for 8 hours or overnight.

The next day, remove the chorizo from the bowl or dish and reserve the wine. Remove the outer casing from the chorizo and cut the sausage into 1/4-inch/5-mm slices. Place the slices in a large, heavy-bottom skillet or flameproof serving dish.

If you are adding the brandy, pour it into a small pan and heat gently. Pour the brandy over the chorizo slices, then stand well back and set alight. When the flames have died down, shake the pan gently and add the reserved wine to the pan, then cook over high heat until almost all of the wine has evaporated.

Serve the chorizo in red wine piping hot, in the dish in which it was cooked, sprinkled with parsley to garnish. Accompany with chunks or slices of bread to mop up the juices and provide wooden toothpicks to spear the pieces of chorizo.

fava beans with serrano ham

ingredients

SERVES 6-8

2 oz/55 g serrano or
 prosciutto, pancetta, or
 rindless smoked lean bacon
4 oz/115 g chorizo sausage,
 outer casing removed
4 tbsp. Spanish olive oil
1 onion, finely chopped
2 garlic cloves, finely chopped
splash of dry white wine
1 lb/450 g frozen fava beans,
 thawed, or about
 3 lb/1.3 kg fresh fava
 beans in their pods,
 shelled to give 1 lb/450 g
1 tbsp. chopped fresh mint or
 dill, plus extra to garnish
pinch of sugar
salt and pepper

method

Using a sharp knife, cut the ham, pancetta, or bacon
into small strips. Cut the chorizo into $^3/_4$-inch/2-cm cubes.
Heat the olive oil in a large, heavy-bottom skillet or
ovenproof dish that has a lid. Add the onion and cook
for 5 minutes, or until softened and starting to brown. If
you are using pancetta or bacon, add it with the onion.
Add the garlic and cook for 30 seconds.

Pour the wine into the skillet, increase the heat, and let
it bubble to evaporate the alcohol, then lower the heat.
Add the fava beans, ham, if using, and the chorizo and
cook for 1–2 minutes, stirring all the time to coat in the oil.

Cover the skillet and let the beans simmer very gently in
the oil, stirring from time to time, for 10–15 minutes, or
until the beans are tender. It may be necessary to add a
little water to the skillet during cooking, so keep an eye
on it and add a splash if the beans appear to become
too dry. Stir in the mint or dill and sugar. Season the dish
with salt and pepper, but taste first as you may find that
it does not need any salt.

Transfer the fava beans to a large, warmed serving dish,
several smaller ones, or individual plates and serve piping
hot, garnished with chopped mint or dill.

serrano ham with arugula

ingredients

SERVES 6

5 oz/140 g arugula, separated
    into leaves
4¹/₂ tbsp. olive oil
1¹/₂ tbsp. orange juice
10 oz/280 g thinly sliced
    serrano ham
salt and pepper

method

Place the arugula in a bowl and pour in the olive oil
and orange juice. Season to taste with salt and pepper
and toss well.

Arrange the slices of ham on individual serving plates,
folding it into attractive shapes. Divide the arugula between
the plates and serve immediately.

tiny spanish meatballs in almond sauce

ingredients

SERVES 6–8

2 oz/55 g white or brown
  bread, crusts removed

3 tbsp. water

1 lb/450 g lean ground pork

1 large onion, finely chopped

1 garlic clove, crushed

2 tbsp. chopped fresh flat-leaf
  parsley, plus extra to garnish

1 egg, beaten

freshly grated nutmeg

salt and pepper

flour, for coating

2 tbsp. Spanish olive oil

squeeze of lemon juice

crusty bread, to serve

almond sauce

2 tbsp. Spanish olive oil

1 oz/25 g white or brown
  bread, torn into pieces

4 oz/115 g blanched almonds

2 garlic cloves, finely chopped

5 fl oz/150 ml/²/₃ cup dry
  white wine

salt and pepper

15 fl oz/425 ml/scant 2 cups
  vegetable stock

method

To prepare the meatballs, soak the bread in the water in a bowl for 5 minutes. With your hands, squeeze out the water and return the bread to the dried bowl. Add the pork, onion, garlic, parsley, and egg, then season well with grated nutmeg and a little salt and pepper. Knead the ingredients well together to form a smooth mixture.

Spread some flour on a plate. With floured hands, shape the meat mixture into about 30 equal-size balls, then roll each meatball in flour until coated.

Heat the olive oil in a large, heavy-bottom skillet and cook the meatballs, in batches, for 4–5 minutes, or until browned on all sides. Using a slotted spoon, remove the meatballs from the skillet and set aside.

To make the almond sauce, heat the olive oil in the skillet. Add the bread and the almonds to the skillet and cook gently, stirring frequently, until golden brown. Add the garlic and cook for an additional 30 seconds, then pour in the wine and boil for 1–2 minutes. Season to taste with salt and pepper and let cool slightly.

Transfer the almond mixture to a food processor. Pour in the vegetable stock and blend the mixture until smooth. Return the sauce to the skillet. Carefully add the cooked meatballs and let simmer for 25 minutes, or until tender. Season the sauce with salt and pepper if necessary.

Transfer the meatballs and almond sauce to a warmed serving dish, add a squeeze of lemon juice to taste, and sprinkle with chopped parsley to garnish. Serve piping hot, with chunks of crusty bread to mop up the sauce.

tiny meatballs with tomato sauce

ingredients

MAKES 60

olive oil

1 red onion, very finely chopped

1 lb 2 oz/500 g fresh ground lamb

1 large egg, beaten

2 tsp. freshly squeezed lemon juice

1/2 tsp. ground cumin

pinch of cayenne pepper, to taste

2 tbsp. very finely chopped fresh mint

salt and pepper

10 fl oz/300 ml/1 1/4 cups tomato & bell pepper salsa (see page 56), to serve

method

Heat 1 tablespoon of olive oil in a skillet over medium heat. Add the onion and cook for 5 minutes, stirring occasionally, until softened but not browned.

Remove the skillet from the heat and let cool. Add the onion to the lamb with the egg, lemon juice, cumin, cayenne, mint, and salt and pepper to taste in a large bowl. Use your hands to squeeze all the ingredients together. Cook a small piece of the mixture and taste to see if the seasoning needs adjusting.

With wet hands, shape the mixture into about 60 x 3/4-inch/2-cm balls. Place on a tray and let chill for at least 20 minutes.

When ready to cook, heat a small amount of olive oil in 1 or 2 large skillets (the exact amount of oil will depend on how much fat is in the lamb). Arrange the meatballs in a single layer, without overcrowding the skillet, and cook over medium heat for 5 minutes, until brown on the outside but still pink inside. Work in batches if necessary, keeping the cooked meatballs warm while you cook the remainder.

Gently reheat the tomato & bell pepper salsa and serve with the meatballs for dipping. These are best served warm with reheated sauce, but they are also enjoyable at room temperature.

mixed tapas platter with beef

ingredients

SERVES 8–10

7 oz/200 g small waxy
potatoes, unpeeled

5 tbsp. olive oil

2 sirloin steaks, about
8 oz/225 g each

1 fresh red chili, seeded and
finely chopped (optional)

12 oz/350 g Queso del
Montsec or other goat
cheese, sliced

6 oz/175 g mixed salad greens

2 tbsp. black olives

2 tbsp. green olives

2 oz/55 g canned anchovies
in oil, drained and halved
lengthwise

1 tbsp. capers, drained and
rinsed

salt and pepper

method

Cook the potatoes in a pan of lightly salted boiling water for
15–20 minutes, or until just tender. Drain and let cool slightly.

Heat a heavy-bottom skillet or grill pan over high heat
and brush with 1 tablespoon of the olive oil. Season the
steaks to taste with pepper and add to the pan. Cook for
1–1 1/2 minutes on each side, or until browned. Reduce
the heat to medium and cook for 1 1/2 minutes on each
side. Remove and rest for 10–15 minutes.

Heat 2 tablespoons of the remaining oil in a skillet. Add
the chili, if using, and the potatoes and cook, turning
frequently, for 10 minutes, or until crisp and golden.

Thinly slice the steaks and arrange the slices alternately
with the cheese slices along the sides of a serving platter.
Mix the salad greens, olives, anchovies, and capers
together, then arrange along the center of the platter.
Drizzle with the remaining oil, then top with the potatoes.
Serve warm or at room temperature.

beef skewers with orange & garlic

ingredients

SERVES 6–8

3 tbsp. white wine

2 tbsp. olive oil

3 garlic cloves, finely chopped

juice of 1 orange

1 lb/450 g rump steak, cubed

1 lb/450 g baby onions, halved

2 orange bell peppers, seeded
    and cut into squares

8 oz/225 g cherry tomatoes,
    halved

salt and pepper

method

Mix the wine, olive oil, garlic, and orange juice together in a shallow, nonmetallic dish. Add the cubes of steak, season to taste with salt and pepper, and toss to coat. Cover with plastic wrap and let marinate in the refrigerator for 2–8 hours.

Preheat the broiler to high. Drain the steak, reserving the marinade. Thread the steak, onions, bell peppers, and tomatoes alternately onto several small skewers – see page 138 for tips on preparing skewers.

Cook the skewers under the hot broiler, turning and brushing frequently with the marinade, for 10 minutes, or until cooked through. Transfer to warmed serving plates and serve immediately.

lamb skewers with lemon

ingredients

SERVES 8

2 garlic cloves, finely chopped

1 Spanish onion, finely chopped

2 tsp. finely grated lemon rind

2 tbsp. lemon juice

1 tsp. fresh thyme leaves

1 tsp. ground coriander

1 tsp. ground cumin

2 tbsp. red wine vinegar

4 fl oz/125 ml/$^1/_2$ cup olive oil

2 lb 4 oz/1 kg lamb fillet, cut
    into $^3/_4$-inch/2-cm pieces

orange or lemon slices,
    to garnish

method

Mix the garlic, onion, lemon rind, lemon juice, thyme, coriander, cumin, vinegar, and olive oil together in a large, shallow, nonmetallic dish, whisking well until thoroughly combined.

Thread the pieces of lamb onto 16 wooden skewers (see page 138 for tips on preparing skewers) and add to the dish, turning well to coat. Cover with plastic wrap and let marinate in the refrigerator for 2–8 hours, turning occasionally.

Preheat the broiler to medium. Drain the skewers, reserving the marinade. Cook under the hot broiler, turning frequently and brushing with the marinade, for 10 minutes, or until tender and cooked to your liking. Serve immediately, garnished with orange slices.

miniature pork brocherres

ingredients

MAKES 12

1 lb/450 g lean boneless pork

3 tbsp. Spanish olive oil, plus
    extra for oiling (optional)

grated rind and juice of
    1 large lemon

2 garlic cloves, crushed

2 tbsp. chopped fresh
    flat-leaf parsley, plus extra
    to garnish

1 tbsp. ras-el-hanout spice
    blend

salt and pepper

method

The brochettes are marinated overnight, so remember to do this in advance in order that they are ready when you need them. Cut the pork into pieces about ³/4 inch/2 cm square and put in a large, shallow, nonmetallic dish that will hold the pieces in a single layer.

To prepare the marinade, put all the remaining ingredients in a bowl and mix well together. Pour the marinade over the pork and toss the meat in it until well coated. Cover the dish and let marinate in the refrigerator for 8 hours or overnight, stirring the pork 2–3 times.

Preheat the broiler, grill pan, or barbecue. Thread 3 marinated pork pieces, leaving a little space between each piece, onto each prepared skewer*. Cook the brochettes for 10–15 minutes, or until tender and lightly charred, turning several times and basting with the remaining marinade during cooking. Serve the pork brochettes piping hot, garnished with parsley.

* You can use wooden or metal skewers to cook the brochettes and for this recipe you will need about 12 x 6-inch/15-cm skewers. If you are using wooden ones, soak them in cold water for about 30 minutes prior to using. This helps to stop them burning and the food sticking to them during cooking. Metal skewers simply need to be greased, and flat ones should be used in preference to round ones to prevent the food on them falling off.

chicken livers in sherry sauce

ingredients

SERVES 6

1 lb/450 g chicken livers
2 tbsp. Spanish olive oil
1 small onion, finely chopped
2 garlic cloves, finely chopped
3¹/₂ fl oz/100 ml/generous
    ¹/₃ cup dry Spanish sherry
salt and pepper
2 tbsp. chopped fresh
    flat-leaf parsley
crusty bread or toast, to serve

method

If necessary, trim the chicken livers, cutting away any ducts and gristle, then cut them into small, bite-size pieces.

Heat the olive oil in a large, heavy-bottom skillet. Add the onion and cook for 5 minutes, or until softened but not browned. Add the garlic and cook for an additional 30 seconds.

Add the chicken livers to the skillet and cook for 2–3 minutes, stirring all the time, until they are firm and have changed color on the outside but are still pink and soft in the center. Using a slotted spoon, lift the chicken livers from the pan, transfer them to a large, warmed serving dish or several smaller ones, and keep warm.

Add the sherry to the skillet, increase the heat, and let it bubble for 3–4 minutes to evaporate the alcohol and reduce slightly. At the same time, deglaze the skillet by scraping and stirring all the bits on the bottom of the skillet into the sauce with a wooden spoon. Season the sauce to taste with salt and pepper.

Pour the sherry sauce over the chicken livers and sprinkle over the parsley. Serve piping hot, accompanied by chunks or slices of crusty bread or toast to mop up the sherry sauce.

chicken rolls with olives

ingredients

SERVES 6–8

4 oz/115 g/²/₃ cup black
olives in oil, drained

5 oz/140 g/1¹/₄ sticks butter,
softened

4 tbsp. chopped fresh parsley

4 skinless, boneless
chicken breasts

2 tbsp. oil from the olive jar

method

Preheat the oven to 400°F/200°C. Pit and chop the olives. Mix half the olives, the butter, and parsley together in a bowl.

Place the chicken breasts between 2 sheets of plastic wrap and beat gently with a meat mallet or the side of rolling pin.

Spread the olive and herb butter over one side of each flattened chicken breast and roll up. Secure with a wooden toothpick or tie with clean string if necessary.

Place the chicken rolls in an ovenproof dish. Drizzle over the oil from the olive jar and bake in the preheated oven for 45–55 minutes, or until tender and the juices run clear when the chicken is pierced with the point of a sharp knife.

Transfer the chicken rolls to a cutting board and discard the cocktail sticks or string. Using a sharp knife, cut into slices, then transfer to warmed serving plates and serve.

chicken in lemon & garlic

ingredients

SERVES 6–8

4 large skinless, boneless
    chicken breasts

5 tbsp. Spanish olive oil

1 onion, finely chopped

6 garlic cloves, finely
    chopped

grated rind of 1 lemon, finely
    pared rind of 1 lemon and
    juice of both lemons

4 tbsp. chopped fresh
    flat-leaf parsley, plus extra
    to garnish

salt and pepper

lemon wedges and crusty
    bread, to serve

method

Using a sharp knife, slice the chicken breasts widthwise into very thin slices. Heat the olive oil in a large, heavy-bottom skillet, add the onion and cook for 5 minutes, or until softened but not browned. Add the garlic and cook for an additional 30 seconds.

Add the sliced chicken to the skillet and cook gently for 5–10 minutes, stirring from time to time, until all the ingredients are lightly browned and the chicken is tender.

Add the grated lemon rind and the lemon juice and let it bubble. At the same time, deglaze the skillet by scraping and stirring all the bits on the bottom of the skillet into the juices with a wooden spoon. Remove the skillet from the heat, stir in the parsley, and season to taste with salt and pepper.

Transfer the chicken in lemon and garlic, piping hot, to a warmed serving dish. Sprinkle with the pared lemon rind, garnish with the parsley, and serve with lemon wedges for squeezing over the chicken, accompanied by chunks or slices of crusty bread for mopping up the lemon and garlic juices.

for seafood fans

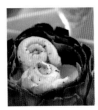

Spain is bordered by the Atlantic and Mediterranean seas, so fresh fish and shellfish are eaten in vast quantities in this country. You only have to pay a visit to a Spanish fish market to see the incredible array of different varieties and, needless to say, they are the pride of Spanish tapas. This chapter has a selection of the best recipes and it is worth spending a little extra on top-quality fresh ingredients, even if it is only on special occasions. When you bite into a chunk of angler fish or a sizzling giant garlic shrimp, you will understand why.

Shrimp are enjoyed throughout the whole of Spain and there will be a shrimp dish or two on almost all tapas menus. Its popularity is very much in evidence in the older-style Spanish tapas bars, and one good reason for this is that, apart from the occasional fork, cutlery is not involved in eating tapas, so shrimp are shelled with enthusiasm and the shell discarded on the floor along with lemon seeds, toothpicks, and paper napkins. A covering of sawdust on the floor is often provided for this very reason!

Many of these dishes work very well as smart, elegant first courses – adjust the quantities if necessary to suit the number of servings you require.

angler fish, rosemary & bacon skewers

ingredients

MAKES 12

12 oz/350 g angler fish tail or
  9 oz/250 g angler fish fillet
12 stalks of fresh rosemary
3 tbsp. Spanish olive oil
juice of 1/2 small lemon
1 garlic clove, crushed
salt and pepper
6 thick slices canadian bacon
lemon wedges, to garnish
aïoli, to serve (see page 70)

method

If using angler fish tail, cut either side of the central bone
with a sharp knife and remove the flesh to form 2 fillets.
Slice the fillets in half lengthwise, then cut each fillet into
12 bite-size chunks to give a total of 24 pieces. Put the
angler fish pieces in a large bowl.

To prepare the rosemary skewers, strip the leaves off the
stalks and set them aside, leaving a few leaves at one end.

For the marinade, finely chop the reserved leaves and
whisk together in a bowl with the olive oil, lemon juice,
garlic, and salt and pepper to taste. Add the angler fish
pieces and toss until coated in the marinade. Cover and
let marinate in the refrigerator for 1–2 hours.

Cut each bacon slice in half lengthwise, then in half
widthwise, and roll up each piece. Thread 2 pieces of
angler fish alternately with 2 bacon rolls onto the prepared
rosemary skewers.

Preheat the broiler, grill pan, or barbecue. If you are
cooking the skewers under a broiler, arrange them on the
broiler pan so that the leaves of the rosemary skewers
protrude from the broiler and therefore do not catch fire
during cooking. Broil the angler fish and bacon skewers
for 10 minutes, turning from time to time and basting with
any remaining marinade, or until cooked. Serve hot,
garnished with lemon wedges for squeezing over them
and accompanied by a bowl of aïoli in which to dip them.

traditional catalan salt cod salad

ingredients

SERVES 4–6

14 oz/400 g dried salt cod
in 1 piece

6 scallions, thinly sliced on
the diagonal

6 tbsp. extra virgin olive oil

1 tbsp. sherry vinegar

1 tbsp. lemon juice

2 large red bell peppers,
broiled, peeled, seeded,
and very finely diced

12 large black olives, pitted
and sliced

2 large, juicy tomatoes,
thinly sliced

pepper

2 tbsp. very finely chopped
fresh parsley, to garnish

method

Place the dried salt cod in a large bowl, then cover with cold water and let soak for 48 hours, changing the water 3 times a day.

Pat the salt cod very dry with paper towels and remove the skin and bones, then use your fingers to tear into fine shreds. Place in a large, nonmetallic bowl with the scallions, olive oil, vinegar, and lemon juice and toss together. Season with pepper, then cover and let marinate in the refrigerator for 3 hours.

Stir in the bell peppers and olives. Taste and adjust the seasoning, if necessary, remembering that the cod and olives might be salty. Arrange the tomato slices on a large serving platter or individual serving plates and spoon the salad on top. Sprinkle with chopped parsley and serve.

cod & caper croquettes

ingredients

MAKES 12

12 oz/350 g white fish fillets,
    such as cod, haddock, or
    angler fish, skinned and
    boned
10 fl oz/300 ml/1¼ cups milk
salt and pepper
4 tbsp. olive oil or
    2 oz/55 g butter
2 oz/55 g/scant ½ cup all-
    purpose flour
4 tbsp. capers, coarsely
    chopped
1 tsp. paprika
1 garlic clove, crushed
1 tsp. lemon juice
3 tbsp. chopped fresh
    flat-leaf parsley, plus extra
    sprigs to garnish
1 egg, beaten
2 oz/55 g/1 cup fresh white
    bread crumbs
1 tbsp. sesame seeds
corn oil, for deep-frying
lemon wedges, to garnish
mayonnaise, to serve

method

Put the fish fillets in a large, heavy-bottom skillet. Add
the milk and season to taste with salt and pepper. Bring to
a boil, then lower the heat, cover the skillet, and cook for
8–10 minutes, or until the fish flakes easily. Carefully
remove the fish, reserving the milk. Flake the fish.

Heat the olive oil or butter in a pan. Stir in the flour to
form a paste and cook gently, stirring, for 1 minute. Remove
the pan from the heat and gradually stir in the reserved
milk until smooth. Return to the heat and slowly bring to
a boil, stirring all the time, until the mixture thickens.

Remove from the heat, add the flaked fish, and beat the
mixture until smooth. Add the capers, paprika, garlic,
lemon juice, and parsley and mix well. Season to taste
with salt and pepper. Transfer the mixture to a dish and
let cool, then cover and refrigerate for 2–3 hours.

Pour the beaten egg onto a plate. Combine the bread
crumbs and sesame seeds on a separate plate. Divide
the fish mixture into 12 portions and, with lightly floured
hands, form each portion into a 3-inch/ 7.5-cm sausage
shape. Dip each croquette in the beaten egg, then coat
it in the bread crumb mixture. Let chill for about 1 hour.

Heat the oil in a deep-fryer to 350–375°F/180–190°C.
Cook the croquettes, in batches, for 3 minutes, or until
golden brown and crispy. Drain well on paper towels.

Serve piping hot, garnished with lemon wedges and parsley
sprigs, and accompanied by a bowl of mayonnaise for dipping.

salt cod & avocado

ingredients

SERVES 6

12 oz/350 g dried salt cod

2 tbsp. olive oil

1 onion, finely chopped

1 garlic clove, finely chopped

3 avocados

1 tbsp. lemon juice

pinch of chili powder

1 tbsp. dry sherry

4 tbsp. heavy cream

salt and pepper

method

Soak the dried salt cod in cold water for 48 hours, changing the water 3 times a day. Drain well and pat dry on paper towels, then chop into large chunks.

Preheat the oven to 350°F/180°C. Heat the olive oil in a large, heavy-bottom skillet. Add the onion and garlic and cook over low heat, stirring occasionally, for 5 minutes, or until softened. Add the fish and cook over medium heat, stirring frequently, for 6–8 minutes, or until the fish flakes easily. Remove the skillet from the heat and let cool slightly.

Meanwhile, halve the avocados lengthwise and remove and discard the pits. Using a teaspoon, carefully scoop out the flesh without piercing the shells. Reserve the shells and mash the flesh with the lemon juice in a bowl.

Remove and discard any skin and bones from the fish, then add the fish mixture to the avocado, together with the chili powder, sherry, and cream. Beat well with a fork and season to taste with salt and pepper.

Spoon the mixture into the avocado shells and place them on a baking sheet. Bake in the preheated oven for 10–15 minutes, then transfer to warmed serving plates and serve.

catalan fish

ingredients

SERVES 4

4 globe artichokes

2 soles, filleted

1/2 lemon

8 fl oz/225 ml/1 cup dry white
wine

2 oz/55 g/1/2 stick butter

2 tbsp. all-purpose flour

8 fl oz/225 ml/1 cup milk

freshly grated nutmeg

1 bay leaf

4 oz/115 g/2 cups sliced
mushrooms

salt and pepper

method

Cut or break off the stems from the artichokes and remove
and discard the tough outer leaves. Trim the points of the
leaves with kitchen scissors. Place the artichokes in a pan
and add enough water to cover and a pinch of salt. Bring
to a boil, then reduce the heat and cook for 30 minutes,
or until tender.

Meanwhile, season the fish fillets to taste with salt and
pepper and squeeze over the lemon. Roll up each fillet
and secure with a wooden toothpick. Place them in a
shallow pan, then pour in the wine and poach gently,
spooning over the wine occasionally, for 15 minutes.

Melt half the butter in a separate pan, then add the flour
and cook, stirring constantly, for 2 minutes, or until golden.
Remove the pan from the heat and gradually stir in the
milk. Return the pan to the heat and bring to a boil, stirring
constantly until thickened and smooth. Reduce the heat
to very low, then season to taste with salt, pepper, and
nutmeg and add the bay leaf.

Melt the remaining butter in a skillet. Add the mushrooms
and cook over medium heat, stirring occasionally, for
3 minutes. Remove the skillet from the heat.

Remove the artichokes from the pan with a slotted spoon
and drain on paper towels. Remove and discard the hairy
chokes and prickly leaves. Place the artichokes on serving
plates. Divide the mushrooms between the artichoke
cavities and spoon in the sauce, removing and discarding
the bay leaf. Transfer the fish fillets to a plate with a slotted
spoon and remove and discard the toothpicks. Place the
fillets in the artichoke cavities and serve.

sardines with lemon & chili

ingredients

SERVES 4

1 lb/450 g fresh sardines, scaled, cleaned, and heads removed

4 tbsp. lemon juice

1 garlic clove, finely chopped

1 tbsp. finely chopped fresh dill

1 tsp. finely chopped fresh red chili

4 tbsp. olive oil

salt and pepper

method

Place the sardines, skin-side up, on a cutting board and press along the length of the spines with your thumbs. Turn them over and remove and discard the bones.

Place the fillets, skin-side down, in a shallow, nonmetallic dish and sprinkle with the lemon juice. Cover with plastic wrap and let stand in a cool place for 30 minutes.

Drain off any excess lemon juice. Sprinkle the garlic, dill, and chili over the fish and season to taste with salt and pepper. Drizzle over the olive oil, then cover with plastic wrap and let chill for 12 hours before serving.

sardines marinated in sherry vinegar

ingredients

SERVES 6

12 small fresh sardines

6 fl oz/175 ml/¾ cup Spanish
    olive oil

4 tbsp. sherry vinegar

2 carrots, cut into julienne
    strips

1 onion, thinly sliced

1 garlic clove, crushed

1 bay leaf

salt and pepper

4 tbsp. chopped fresh
    flat-leaf parsley

few sprigs of fresh dill,
    to garnish

lemon wedges, to serve

method

If it has not already been done, clean the fish by scraping the scales off with a knife, being careful not to cut the skin. The choice is yours whether you then leave the heads and tails on or cut them off and discard. Slit along the belly of each fish and remove the innards under cold running water. Then, dry each fish well on paper towels.

Heat 4 tablespoons of the olive oil in a large, heavy-bottom skillet. Add the sardines and cook for 10 minutes, or until browned on both sides. Using a spatula, very carefully remove the sardines from the skillet and transfer to a large, shallow, nonmetallic dish that will hold the sardines in a single layer.

Gently heat the remaining olive oil and the sherry vinegar in a large pan, add the carrot strips, onion, garlic, and bay leaf and let simmer gently for 5 minutes, until softened. Season the vegetables to taste with salt and pepper. Let the mixture cool slightly, then pour the marinade over the sardines.

Cover the dish and let the sardines cool before transferring to the refrigerator. Let marinate for about 8 hours or overnight, spooning the marinade over the sardines occasionally, although there is no necessity to get up in the middle of the night! Return the sardines to room temperature before serving, sprinkle with parsley, and garnish with dill sprigs. Serve with lemon wedges.

sardines with romesco sauce

ingredients

SERVES 6

24 fresh sardines, scaled,
    cleaned, and heads
    removed
4 oz/115 g/generous 3/4 cup
    all-purpose flour
4 eggs, lightly beaten
9 oz/250 g fresh white bread
    crumbs
6 tbsp. chopped fresh parsley
4 tbsp. chopped fresh marjoram
vegetable oil, for deep-frying

romesco sauce

1 red bell pepper, halved
    and seeded
2 tomatoes, halved
4 garlic cloves
4 fl oz/125 ml/1/2 cup olive oil
1 slice white bread, diced
4 tbsp. blanched almonds
1 fresh red chili, seeded
    and chopped
2 shallots, chopped
1 tsp. paprika
2 tbsp. red wine vinegar
2 tsp. sugar
1 tbsp. water

method

First make the sauce. Preheat the oven to 425°F/220°C.
Place the bell pepper, tomatoes, and garlic in an
ovenproof dish and drizzle over 1 tablespoon of the olive
oil, turning to coat. Bake in the preheated oven for
20–25 minutes, then remove from the oven and cool.
When cool enough to handle, peel off their skins and
place the flesh in a food processor.

Heat 1 tablespoon of the remaining oil in a skillet. Add
the bread and almonds and cook over low heat for a few
minutes until browned. Remove and drain on paper
towels. Add the chili, shallots, and paprika to the pan
and cook for 5 minutes, or until the shallots are softened.

Transfer the almond mixture and shallot mixture to the
food processor and add the vinegar, sugar, and water.
Process to a paste. With the motor still running, gradually
add the remaining oil through the feeder tube. Transfer
to a bowl, cover, and reserve.

Place the sardines, skin-side up, on a cutting board and
press along the length of the spines with your thumbs.
Turn over and remove and discard the bones. Place the
flour and eggs in separate bowls. Mix the bread crumbs
and herbs together in a third bowl. Toss the fish in the
flour, the eggs, then in the bread crumbs.

Heat the vegetable oil in a large pan to 350–375°F/
180–190°C, or until a cube of bread browns in 30
seconds. Deep-fry the fish for 4–5 minutes, or until
golden and tender. Drain and serve with the sauce.

pickled mackerel

ingredients

SERVES 6

8 fresh mackerel fillets

10 fl oz/300 ml/1¼ cups
    extra-virgin olive oil

2 large red onions, thinly
    sliced

2 carrots, sliced

2 bay leaves

2 garlic cloves, thinly sliced

2 dried red chilies

1 fennel bulb, halved and
    thinly sliced

10 fl oz/300 ml/1¼ cups
    sherry vinegar

1½ tbsp. coriander seeds

salt and pepper

toasted French bread slices,
    to serve

method

Preheat the broiler to medium. Place the mackerel fillets, skin-side up, on a broiler rack and brush with oil. Broil under the hot broiler, about 4 inches/10 cm from the heat source, for 4–6 minutes, until the skins become brown and crispy and the flesh flakes easily. Reserve until required.

Heat the remaining oil in a large skillet. Add the onions and cook for 5 minutes until softened but not browned. Add the remaining ingredients and let simmer for 10 minutes until the carrots are tender.

Flake the mackerel flesh into large pieces, removing the skin and tiny bones. Place the mackerel pieces in a preserving jar and pour over the onion, carrot, and fennel mixture. (The jar should accommodate everything packed in quite tightly with the minimum air gap at the top once the vegetable mixture has been poured in.) Let cool completely, then cover tightly and let chill for at least 24 hours and up to 5 days. Serve the pieces of mackerel on toasted slices of French bread with a little of the oil drizzled over.

Alternatively, serve the mackerel and its pickled vegetables as a first-course salad.

fresh salmon in mojo sauce

ingredients

SERVES 8

4 fresh salmon fillets,
weighing about
1 lb 10 oz/750 g in total
salt and pepper
3 tbsp. Spanish olive oil
1 fresh flat-leaf parsley sprig,
to garnish

for the mojo sauce

2 garlic cloves, peeled
2 tsp. paprika
1 tsp. ground cumin
5 tbsp. Spanish extra-virgin
olive oil
2 tbsp. white wine vinegar
salt

method

To prepare the Mojo Sauce, put the garlic, paprika, and cumin in the bowl of a food processor fitted with the metal blade and, using a pulsing action, blend for 1 minute to mix well together. With the motor still running, add 1 tablespoon of the olive oil, drop by drop, through the feeder tube. When it has been added, scrape down the sides of the bowl with a spatula, then very slowly continue to pour in the oil in a thin, steady stream, until all the oil has been added and the sauce has slightly thickened. Add the vinegar and blend for an additional 1 minute. Season the sauce with salt to taste.

To prepare the salmon, remove the skin, cut each fillet in half widthwise, then cut lengthwise into 3/4-inch/2-cm thick slices, discarding any bones. Season the pieces of fish to taste with salt and pepper.

Heat the olive oil in a large, heavy-bottom skillet. When hot, add the pieces of fish and cook for about 10 minutes, depending on its thickness, turning occasionally until cooked and browned on both sides.

Transfer the salmon to a warmed serving dish, drizzle over some of the Mojo Sauce, and serve hot, garnished with parsley, and accompanied by the remaining sauce in a small serving bowl.

tuna, egg & potato salad

ingredients

SERVES 4

12 oz/350 g new potatoes,
    unpeeled
1 hard-cooked egg, cooled
    and shelled
3 tbsp. olive oil
1¹/₂ tbsp. white wine vinegar
4 oz/115 g canned tuna in oil,
    drained and flaked
2 shallots, finely chopped
1 tomato, peeled and diced
2 tbsp. chopped fresh parsley
salt and pepper

method

Cook the potatoes in a pan of lightly salted boiling water for 10 minutes, then remove from the heat, cover, and let stand for 15–20 minutes, or until tender.

Meanwhile, slice the egg, then cut each slice in half. Whisk the olive oil and vinegar together in a bowl and season to taste with salt and pepper. Spoon a little of the vinaigrette into a serving dish to coat the base.

Drain the potatoes, then peel and thinly slice. Place half the slices over the base of the dish and season to taste with salt, then top with half the tuna, half the egg slices, and half the shallots. Pour over half the remaining dressing. Make a second layer with the remaining potato slices, tuna, egg, and shallots, then pour over the remaining dressing.

Finally, top the salad with the tomato and parsley. Cover with plastic wrap and let stand in a cool place for 1–2 hours before serving.

tuna with pimiento-stuffed olives

ingredients

SERVES 6

2 fresh tuna steaks, weighing
about 9 oz/250 g in total
and about 1 inch/2.5 cm
thick

5 tbsp. Spanish olive oil

3 tbsp. red wine vinegar

4 sprigs of fresh thyme, plus
extra to garnish

1 bay leaf

salt and pepper

2 tbsp. all-purpose flour

1 onion, finely chopped

2 garlic cloves, finely chopped

3 oz/85 g/1/2 cup pimiento-
stuffed green olives, sliced

crusty bread, to serve

method

Don't get caught out with this recipe—the tuna steaks
need to be marinated, so remember to start preparing
the dish the day before you are going to serve it. Remove
the skin from the tuna steaks, then cut the steaks in half
along the grain of the fish. Cut each half into 1/2-inch/1-cm
thick slices against the grain.

Put 3 tablespoons of the olive oil and the vinegar in a large,
shallow, nonmetallic dish. Strip the leaves from the sprigs
of thyme and add these to the dish with the bay leaf and
salt and pepper to taste. Add the prepared strips of tuna,
cover the dish, and let marinate in the refrigerator for
8 hours or overnight.

The next day, put the flour in a plastic bag. Remove the
tuna strips from the marinade, reserving the marinade
for later, add them to the bag of flour and toss well until
they are lightly coated.

Heat the remaining olive oil in a large, heavy-bottom skillet.
Add the onion and garlic and gently cook for 5–10 minutes,
or until softened and golden brown. Add the tuna strips
to the skillet and cook for 2–5 minutes, turning several
times, until the fish becomes opaque. Add the reserved
marinade and olives to the skillet and cook for an
additional 1–2 minutes, stirring, until the fish is tender
and the sauce has thickened.

Serve the tuna and olives piping hot, garnished with
thyme sprigs. Accompany with chunks or slices of crusty
bread for mopping up the sauce.

tuna rolls

ingredients

SERVES 4

3 red bell peppers
4 fl oz/125 ml/1/2 cup olive oil
2 tbsp. lemon juice
5 tbsp. red wine vinegar
2 garlic cloves, finely chopped
1 tsp. paprika
1 tsp. dried chili flakes
2 tsp. sugar
2 tbsp. salted capers
7 oz/200 g canned tuna in oil,
    drained and flaked

method

Preheat the broiler to high. Place the bell peppers on a baking sheet and cook under the preheated broiler, turning frequently, for 10 minutes, until the skin is blackened and blistered all over. Using tongs, transfer to a plastic bag, then tie the top and let cool.

Meanwhile, whisk the olive oil, lemon juice, vinegar, garlic, paprika, chili flakes, and sugar together in a small bowl.

When the peppers are cool enough to handle, peel off the skins, then cut the flesh into thirds lengthwise and seed. Place the pepper pieces in a nonmetallic dish and pour over the dressing, turning to coat. Let stand in a cool place for 30 minutes.

Rub the salt off the capers and mix with the tuna. Drain the pepper pieces, reserving the dressing. Divide the tuna mixture between the pepper pieces and roll up. Secure with a wooden toothpick. Place the tuna rolls on a serving platter, then spoon over the dressing and serve at room temperature.

empanadillas

ingredients

SERVES 6–8

2 tbsp. olive oil, plus extra
    for brushing

1 lb 2 oz/500 g fresh spinach
    leaves

2 garlic cloves, finely
    chopped

8 canned anchovy fillets in
    oil, drained and chopped

2 tbsp. raisins, soaked in hot
    water for 10 minutes

1½ oz/40 g/scant ⅓ cup
    pine nuts

1 lb/450 g puff pastry, thawed
    if frozen

all-purpose flour, for dusting

1 egg, lightly beaten

salt and pepper

method

Preheat the oven to 350°F/180°C. Lightly brush 1–2 baking sheets with olive oil.

Trim and discard any tough stems from the spinach and finely chop the leaves.

Heat the olive oil in a large pan. Add the chopped spinach, then cover and cook over low heat, gently shaking the pan occasionally, for 3 minutes. Stir in the garlic and anchovies and cook, uncovered, for an additional 1 minute. Remove the pan from the heat.

Drain the raisins and chop, then stir them into the spinach mixture with the pine nuts and salt and pepper to taste. Let cool.

Roll out the pastry on a lightly floured counter to a circle about ⅛ inch/3 mm thick. Stamp out circles using a 3-inch/7.5-cm biscuit cutter. Re-roll the trimmings and stamp out more circles.

Place 1–2 heaped teaspoonfuls of the spinach filling onto each pastry round. Brush the edges with water and fold over to make half moons. Press together well to seal. Place the empanadillas on the baking sheets and brush with beaten egg to glaze, then bake in the preheated oven for 15 minutes, or until golden brown. Serve warm.

squid & beans

ingredients

SERVES 6

1 lb 2 oz/500 g prepared squid

3 garlic cloves, chopped

10 fl oz/300 ml/1 1/4 cups dry
    red wine

1 lb 2 oz/500 g new potatoes,
    unpeeled

225 g/8 oz green beans, cut
    into short lengths

4 tbsp. olive oil

1 tbsp. red wine vinegar

salt and pepper

method

Preheat the oven to 350°F/180°C. Using a sharp knife,
cut the squid into rings about 1/2 inch/1 cm thick and
place them in an ovenproof dish. Sprinkle with half the
garlic, then pour over the wine and season to taste with
salt and pepper. Cover the dish with foil and bake in the
preheated oven for 45–50 minutes, or until the squid
feels tender when pierced with the point of a sharp knife.

Meanwhile, cook the potatoes in a pan of lightly salted
boiling water for 15–20 minutes, or until tender. Drain
and let cool slightly, then thickly slice and place in a
large bowl.

Cook the beans in a separate pan of lightly salted boiling
water for 3–5 minutes, or until tender. Drain and add to
the potatoes. Drain the squid and add to the bowl.

Whisk the olive oil, vinegar, and remaining garlic together
in a bowl and season to taste with salt and pepper. Pour
the dressing over the salad and toss lightly. Divide the
salad between individual serving plates and serve warm.

calamares

ingredients

SERVES 6

1 lb/450 g prepared squid

all-purpose flour, for coating

corn oil, for deep-frying

salt

lemon wedges, to garnish

aïoli, to serve (see page 70)

method

Slice the squid into $^{1}/_{2}$-inch/1-cm rings and halve the tentacles if large. Rinse and dry well on paper towels so that they do not spit during cooking. Dust the squid rings with flour so that they are lightly coated. Do not season the flour, as Spanish cooks will tell you that seasoning squid with salt before cooking toughens it. They should know!

Heat the corn oil in a deep-fryer to 350–375°F/180–190°C, or until a cube of bread browns in 30 seconds. Carefully add the squid rings, in batches so that the temperature of the oil does not drop, and deep-fry for 2–3 minutes, or until golden brown and crisp all over, turning several times. Do not overcook as the squid will become tough and rubbery rather than moist and tender.

Using a slotted spoon, remove the deep-fried squid from the deep-fryer and drain well on paper towels. Transfer to a warm oven while you deep-fry the remaining squid rings.

Sprinkle the deep-fried squid with salt and serve piping hot, garnished with lemon wedges for squeezing over them. Accompany with a bowl of aïoli in which to dip the pieces.

giant garlic shrimp

ingredients

SERVES 4

4 fl oz/125 ml/$^1/_2$ cup olive oil

4 garlic cloves, finely
    chopped

2 hot fresh red chilies, seeded
    and finely chopped

1 lb/450 g cooked jumbo
    shrimp

2 tbsp. chopped fresh
    flat-leaf parsley

salt and pepper

lemon wedges, to garnish

crusty bread, to serve

method

Heat the olive oil in a preheated wok or large, heavy-bottom skillet over low heat. Add the garlic and chilies and cook, stirring occasionally, for 1–2 minutes, until softened but not colored.

Add the shrimp and stir-fry for 2–3 minutes, or until heated through and coated in the oil and garlic mixture.

Turn off the heat and add the chopped parsley, stirring well to mix. Season to taste with salt and pepper.

Divide the shrimp and garlic-flavored oil between warmed serving dishes and garnish with lemon wedges. Serve with lots of crusty bread.

lime-drizzled shrimp

ingredients

SERVES 6

4 limes

12 raw jumbo shrimp, in
their shells

3 tbsp. Spanish olive oil

2 garlic cloves, finely
chopped

splash of fino sherry

salt and pepper

4 tbsp. chopped fresh
flat-leaf parsley

method

Grate the rind and squeeze the juice from 2 of the limes. Cut
the remaining 2 limes into wedges and set aside for later.

To prepare the shrimp, remove the head and legs, leaving
the shells and tails intact. Using a sharp knife, make a
shallow slit along the underside of each shrimp, then
pull out the dark vein and discard. Rinse the shrimp
under cold water and dry well on paper towels.

Heat the olive oil in a large, heavy-bottom skillet, then add
the garlic and cook for 30 seconds. Add the shrimp and
cook for 5 minutes, stirring from time to time, or until they
turn pink and start to curl. Mix in the lime rind, juice, and
a splash of sherry to moisten, then stir well together.

Transfer the cooked shrimp to a serving dish, season to
taste with salt and pepper, and sprinkle with the parsley.
Serve piping hot, accompanied by the reserved lime wedges
for squeezing over the shrimp.

shrimp with saffron dressing

ingredients

SERVES 6–8

large pinch of saffron threads

2 tbsp. warm water

5 fl oz/150 ml/$^2/_3$ cup
	mayonnaise

2 tbsp. grated onion

4 tbsp. lemon juice

1 tsp. Dijon mustard

2 lb 4 oz/1 kg cooked
	Mediterranean shrimp

1 romaine lettuce, separated
	into leaves

4 tomatoes, cut into wedges

8 black olives

salt and pepper

method

Stir the saffron with the water in a small bowl. Mix the mayonnaise, onion, lemon juice, and mustard together in a separate, nonmetallic bowl, whisking gently until thoroughly combined. Season to taste with salt and pepper and stir in the saffron soaking liquid. Cover with plastic wrap and let chill until required.

Pull the heads off the shrimp and peel. Cut along the length of the back of each shrimp and remove and discard the dark vein. Rinse and pat dry with paper towels.

Arrange the lettuce leaves on a large serving platter or on individual serving plates. Top with the shrimp and scatter with the tomato wedges and olives. Serve with the saffron dressing.

garlic shrimp with lemon and parsley

ingredients

SERVES 6

60 raw jumbo shrimp, thawed
　　if using frozen

5 fl oz/150 ml/²/₃ cup olive oil

6 garlic cloves, thinly sliced

3 dried hot red chilies
　　(optional)

6 tbsp. freshly squeezed
　　lemon juice

6 tbsp. very finely chopped
　　fresh parsley

french bread, to serve

method

Peel and devein the shrimp and remove the heads,
leaving the tails on. Rinse and pat the shrimp dry.

Heat the olive oil in a large, deep sauté pan or skillet.
Add the garlic and chilies, if using, and stir constantly
until they begin to sizzle. Add the shrimp and cook until
they turn pink and begin to curl.

Use a slotted spoon to transfer the shrimp to warm
earthenware bowls. Sprinkle each bowl with lemon juice
and parsley. Serve with plenty of bread to mop up the juices.

cidered scallops

ingredients

SERVES 4–5

1¾ pints/1 litre/4 cups dry
    cider
4 tbsp. lemon juice
20 shelled scallops
3 oz/85 g/¾ stick butter
2 tbsp. all-purpose flour
8 fl oz/225 ml/1 cup sour
    cream
4 oz/115 g white mushrooms
salt and pepper

method

Preheat the oven to 225°F/110°C. Pour the cider and lemon juice into a large, shallow pan and season to taste with salt and pepper. Add the scallops and poach for 10 minutes, or until tender. Using a slotted spoon, transfer the scallops to an ovenproof dish. Dot with 2 tablespoons of the butter, then cover with foil and keep warm in the oven.

Bring the scallop cooking liquid to a boil and continue to boil until reduced by about half. Mix together 2 tablespoons of the remaining butter and the flour, mashing well with a fork to make a paste. Beat the paste, a little at a time, into the liquid until thickened and smooth. Stir in the sour cream and simmer gently for 5–10 minutes.

Taste the sauce and adjust the seasoning if necessary. Remove the scallops from the oven and return them to the pan, then heat through for 2–3 minutes.

Meanwhile, melt the remaining butter in a small skillet. Add the mushrooms and cook over low heat, stirring frequently, for 2–3 minutes. Add them to the pan of scallops, then transfer to individual serving dishes and serve.

baked scallops

ingredients

SERVES 4

1 lb 9 oz/700 g shelled
 scallops, chopped

2 onions, finely chopped

2 garlic cloves, finely chopped

3 tbsp. chopped fresh parsley

pinch of freshly grated nutmeg

pinch of ground cloves

2 tbsp. fresh white bread
 crumbs

2 tbsp. olive oil

salt and pepper

method

Preheat the oven to 400°F/200°C. Mix the scallops, onions, garlic, 2 tablespoons of the parsley, the nutmeg, and cloves together in a bowl and season to taste with salt and pepper.

Divide the mixture between 4 scrubbed scallop shells or heatproof dishes. Sprinkle the bread crumbs and remaining parsley on top and drizzle with the olive oil.

Bake the scallops in the preheated oven for 15–20 minutes, or until lightly golden and piping hot. Serve immediately.

scallops in saffron sauce

ingredients

SERVES 8

5 fl oz/150 ml/²/₃ cup dry
    white wine

5 fl oz/150 ml/²/₃ cup fish
    stock

large pinch of saffron threads

2 lb/900 g shelled scallops,
    preferably large ones

salt and pepper

3 tbsp. Spanish olive oil

1 small onion, finely chopped

2 garlic cloves, finely chopped

5 fl oz/150 ml/²/₃ cup heavy
    cream

squeeze of lemon juice

chopped fresh flat-leaf
    parsley, to garnish

crusty bread, to serve

method

Put the wine, fish stock, and saffron in a pan and bring to a boil. Lower the heat, cover, and let simmer gently for 15 minutes.

Meanwhile, remove and discard from each scallop the tough, white muscle that is found opposite the coral, and separate the coral from the scallop. Slice the scallops vertically into thick slices, including the corals if they are present. Dry the scallops well on paper towels, then season to taste with salt and pepper.

Heat the olive oil in a large, heavy-bottom skillet. Add the onion and garlic and cook for 5 minutes, or until softened and lightly browned. Add the sliced scallops to the skillet and cook gently for 5 minutes, stirring occasionally, or until they turn just opaque. The secret is not to overcook the scallops, otherwise they will become tough and rubbery.

Using a slotted spoon, remove the scallops from the skillet and transfer to a warmed plate. Add the saffron liquid to the skillet, bring to a boil, and boil rapidly until reduced to about half. Lower the heat and gradually stir in the cream, just a little at a time. Let simmer gently until the sauce thickens.

Return the scallops to the skillet and let simmer for 1–2 minutes just to heat them through. Add a squeeze of lemon juice and season to taste with salt and pepper. Serve the scallops hot, garnished with the parsley, and accompanied by chunks or slices of crusty bread to mop up the saffron sauce.

seared scallops

ingredients

SERVES 4–6

4 tbsp. olive oil

3 tbsp. orange juice

2 tsp. hazelnut oil

24 shelled scallops

salad greens (optional)

6 oz/175 g cabrales or other
    bleu cheese, crumbled

2 tbsp. chopped fresh dill

salt and pepper

method

Whisk 3 tablespoons of the olive oil, the orange juice, and hazelnut oil together in a pitcher and season to taste with salt and pepper.

Heat the remaining olive oil in a large, heavy-bottom skillet. Add the scallops and cook over high heat for 1 minute on each side, or until golden.

Transfer the scallops to a bed of salad greens or individual plates. Scatter over the cheese and dill, then drizzle with the dressing. Serve warm.

scallops with serrano ham

ingredients

SERVES 4

2 tbsp. lemon juice

3 tbsp. olive oil

2 garlic cloves, finely chopped

1 tbsp. chopped fresh parsley

12 shelled scallops,
    preferably with corals

16 wafer-thin slices
    serrano ham

pepper

method

Mix the lemon juice, olive oil, garlic, and parsley together in a nonmetallic dish. Separate the corals, if using, from the scallops and add both to the dish, turning to coat. Cover with plastic wrap and let marinate at room temperature for 20 minutes.

Preheat the broiler to medium. Drain the scallops, reserving the marinade. Scrunch up a slice of ham and thread it onto a metal skewer, followed by a scallop and a coral, if using. Repeat to fill 4 skewers each with the ham, scallops, and corals, finishing with a scrunched-up slice of ham.

Cook under the hot broiler, basting with the marinade and turning frequently, for 5 minutes, or until the scallops are tender and the ham is crisp.

Transfer to warmed serving plates and sprinkle them with pepper. Spoon over the cooking juices from the broiler pan and serve.

crab with almonds

ingredients

SERVES 4

1 lb/450 g fresh, canned, or
   frozen crabmeat, thawed
4 oz/115 g/1 stick butter
3 oz/85 g slivered almonds
4 fl oz/125 ml/$\frac{1}{2}$ cup heavy
   cream
1 tbsp. chopped fresh parsley
salt and pepper

method

Pick over the crabmeat to remove any pieces of cartilage or shell. Melt half the butter in a heavy-bottom skillet. Add the crabmeat and cook over medium heat, stirring occasionally, for 10 minutes, or until browned. Remove the skillet from the heat and reserve.

Melt the remaining butter in a separate skillet. Add the almonds and cook over low heat, stirring occasionally, for 5 minutes, or until golden brown.

Stir the almonds into the crabmeat and season to taste with salt and pepper. Stir in the cream and parsley and bring to a boil. Reduce the heat and simmer for 3 minutes. Transfer to a warmed serving dish and serve immediately.

clams with fava beans

ingredients

SERVES 4–6

4 canned anchovy fillets
    in oil, drained

1 tsp. salted capers

3 tbsp. olive oil

1 tbsp. sherry vinegar

1 tsp. Dijon mustard

1 lb 2 oz/500 g fresh clams

about 6 fl oz/175 ml/³/₄ cup
    water

1 lb 2 oz/500 g fava beans,
    shelled if fresh

2 tbsp. chopped mixed fresh
    herbs, such as parsley,
    chives, and mint

salt and pepper

method

Place the anchovies in a small bowl, then add water to cover and let soak for 5 minutes. Drain well, then pat dry with paper towels and place in a mortar. Brush the salt off the capers, then add to the mortar and pound to a paste with a pestle.

Whisk the olive oil, vinegar, and mustard together in a separate bowl, then whisk in the anchovy paste and season to taste with salt and pepper. Cover with plastic wrap and let stand at room temperature until required.

Scrub the clams under cold running water. Discard any with broken shells or any that do not close immediately when sharply tapped with the back of a knife. Place the clams in a large, heavy-bottom pan and add the water. Cover and bring to a boil over high heat. Cook, shaking the pan occasionally, for 3–5 minutes, or until the clams have opened. Discard any that remain closed.

Meanwhile, bring a large pan of lightly salted water to a boil. Add the fava beans, then return to a boil and blanch for 5 minutes. Drain, then refresh under cold running water and drain well again. Remove and discard the outer skins and place the fava beans in a bowl.

Drain the clams and remove them from their shells. Add to the beans and sprinkle with the herbs. Add the anchovy vinaigrette and toss lightly. Serve warm.

# of eggs and cheese

Egg-based dishes feature in all tapas menus, and one of the most familiar of these is the delectable Spanish Tortilla – made hearty with the addition of chunks of waxy potato, this is definitely an omelet with attitude! The potatoes can be boiled before being mixed with the eggs, but to make a really authentic tortilla they are first cooked slowly in a generous quantity of olive oil so that they absorb the flavor of the oil but do not become browned or crisp, or fall apart. This chapter includes a recipe for the simplest – and perhaps the best – of tortillas, as well as a few with added extras. There are also recipes for other ways of using eggs – deviled, fried, scrambled, and oven-baked. With their exotic names, such as Flamenco Eggs and Basque Scrambled Eggs, these dishes conjure up wonderful images of Spain.

Cheese dishes are also popular in tapas menus, and some very tempting recipes are given here. If you really want to impress, serve an intriguing combination of fresh figs, crumbly blue cheese, and caramelized almonds. Or try melt-in-the-mouth cheese puffs with a fiery salsa, or tiny empanadillas filled with cheese and olives. It can be difficult to find Spanish cheese on sale in other countries, so alternatives are suggested in case you are unable to source the real thing.

tortilla espanola

ingredients

SERVES 8

1 lb/450 g waxy potatoes

12 fl oz/450 ml/scant 2 cups
  Spanish olive oil

2 onions, chopped

2 large eggs

salt and pepper

sprigs of fresh flat-leaf
  parsley, to garnish

method

Peel the potatoes, cut into small cubes or wedges, then dry well on a clean dish towel. Heat the olive oil in a large, heavy-bottom skillet. Add the potatoes and onions, then lower the heat and cook for about 20 minutes, stirring frequently so that the potato pieces do not clump together, until they are tender but not browned or crisp.

Meanwhile, beat the eggs lightly in a large bowl and season well with salt and pepper. Drain the cooked potatoes and onions in a strainer over a large bowl so that the bowl catches the oil. Set the oil aside. Gently stir the drained potatoes and onions into the beaten eggs.

Wipe the skillet clean then heat 2 tablespoons of the reserved olive oil. When hot, add the egg and potato mixture, lower the heat and cook for 3–5 minutes, or until the underside is just set. Push the potatoes down into the egg to keep them submerged and keep loosening the tortilla from the bottom of the skillet to stop it sticking.

To cook the second side of the tortilla, cover it with a plate. Holding the plate in place, drain off the oil in the skillet, then quickly turn the skillet upside down so that the tortilla falls on to the plate. Return the skillet to the heat and add a little more of the reserved oil if necessary. Slide the tortilla, cooked side uppermost, back into the skillet and continue to cook for 3–5 minutes, or until set underneath. The tortilla is cooked when it is firm and crisp on the outside but still slightly runny in the center.

Slide the tortilla onto a serving plate and let stand for about 15 minutes. Serve it warm or cold, cut into small pieces, garnished with parsley sprigs.

chorizo & cheese tortilla

ingredients

SERVES 8

2 small potatoes

4 tbsp. olive oil

1 small onion, chopped

1 red bell pepper, seeded
    and chopped

2 tomatoes, seeded and
    diced

5 oz/140 g chorizo sausage,
    finely chopped

8 large eggs

2 tbsp. cold water

2 oz/55 g mature mahon,
    manchego, or parmesan
    cheese, grated

salt and pepper

method

Cook the potatoes in a small pan of lightly salted boiling water for 15–20 minutes, or until just tender. Drain and let stand until cool enough to handle, then dice.

Heat the olive oil in a large skillet that can safely be placed under the broiler. Add the onion, bell pepper, and tomatoes and cook over low heat, stirring occasionally, for 5 minutes. Add the diced potatoes and chorizo and cook for an additional 5 minutes. Meanwhile, preheat the broiler to high.

Beat the eggs with the water and salt and pepper to taste in a large bowl. Pour the mixture into the skillet and cook for 8–10 minutes, or until the underside is set. Lift the edge of the tortilla occasionally to let the uncooked egg run underneath. Sprinkle the grated cheese over the tortilla and place under the hot broiler for 3 minutes, or until the top is set and the cheese has melted. Serve, warm or cold, cut into thin wedges.

spinach & mushroom tortilla

ingredients

SERVES 4

2 tbsp. olive oil

3 shallots, finely chopped

12 oz/350 g mushrooms, sliced

10 oz/280 g fresh spinach leaves, coarse stems removed

2 oz/55 g toasted slivered almonds

5 eggs

2 tbsp. chopped fresh parsley

2 tbsp. cold water

3 oz/85 g mature mahon, manchego, or parmesan cheese, grated

salt and pepper

method

Heat the olive oil in a skillet that can safely be placed under the broiler. Add the shallots and cook over low heat, stirring occasionally, for 5 minutes, or until softened. Add the mushrooms and cook, stirring frequently, for an additional 4 minutes. Add the spinach, then increase the heat to medium and cook, stirring frequently, for 3–4 minutes, or until wilted. Reduce the heat, then season to taste with salt and pepper and stir in the slivered almonds.

Beat the eggs with the parsley, water, and salt and pepper to taste in a bowl. Pour the mixture into the skillet and cook for 5–8 minutes, or until the underside is set. Lift the edge of the tortilla occasionally to let the uncooked egg run underneath. Meanwhile, preheat the broiler to high.

Sprinkle the grated cheese over the tortilla and cook under the preheated hot broiler for 3 minutes, or until the top is set and the cheese has melted. Serve, lukewarm or cold, cut into thin wedges.

oven-baked tortilla

ingredients

MAKES 48

olive oil

1 large garlic clove, crushed

4 scallions, white and green
    parts finely chopped

1 green bell pepper, seeded
    and finely diced

1 red bell pepper, seeded
    and finely diced

6 oz/175 g potato, boiled,
    peeled, and diced

5 large eggs

3¹/₂ fl oz/100 ml/scant ¹/₂ cup
    sour cream

6 oz/175 g freshly grated
    Spanish roncal cheese, or
    cheddar or parmesan
    cheese

3 tbsp. snipped fresh chives

salt and pepper

green salad, to serve

method

Preheat the oven to 375°F/190°C. Line a 7 x 10-inch/
18 x 25-cm baking sheet with foil and brush with the
olive oil. Reserve.

Place a little olive oil, the garlic, scallions, and bell
peppers in a skillet and cook over medium heat,
stirring, for 10 minutes, or until the onions are
softened but not browned. Let cool, then stir in the
potato.

Beat the eggs, sour cream, cheese, and chives together
in a large bowl. Stir the cooled vegetables into the bowl
and season to taste with salt and pepper.

Pour the mixture into the baking sheet and smooth over
the top. Bake in the preheated oven for 30–40 minutes,
or until golden brown, puffed and set in the center. Remove
from the oven and let cool and set. Run a spatula around
the edge, then invert onto a cutting board, browned-side
up, and peel off the foil. If the surface looks a little runny,
place it under a medium broiler to dry out.

Let cool completely. Trim the edges if necessary, then cut
into 48 squares. Serve on a platter with wooden toothpicks,
or secure each square to a slice of bread, and accompany
with a green salad.

stuffed eggs

ingredients

SERVES 6

6 hard-cooked eggs, cooled
    and shelled
4¼ oz/120 g canned sardines
    in olive oil, drained
4 tbsp. lemon juice
dash of tabasco sauce
1–2 tbsp. mayonnaise
2 oz/55 g/⅓ cup all-purpose
    flour
3 oz/85 g/1½ cups fresh
    white bread crumbs
1 large egg, lightly beaten
vegetable oil, for deep-frying
salt and pepper
fresh parsley sprigs, to garnish

method

Cut the eggs in half lengthwise and, using a teaspoon, carefully scoop out the yolks into a fine strainer, reserving the egg white halves. Rub the yolks through the strainer into a bowl.

Mash the sardines with a fork, then mix with the egg yolks. Stir in the lemon juice and Tabasco, then add enough mayonnaise to make a paste. Season to taste with salt and pepper.

Spoon the filling into the egg white halves, mounding it up well. Spread out the flour and bread crumbs in separate shallow dishes. Dip each egg half first in the flour, then in the beaten egg and finally in the bread crumbs.

Heat the vegetable oil for deep-frying in a deep-fat fryer or large pan to 350–375°F/180–190°C, or until a cube of bread browns in 30 seconds. Deep-fry the egg halves, in batches if necessary, for 2 minutes, or until golden brown. Drain on paper towels and serve hot, garnished with parsley sprigs.

deviled eggs

ingredients

MAKES 16

8 large eggs

2 whole pimientos (sweet red
    peppers) from a jar or can

8 green olives

5 tbsp. mayonnaise

8 drops tabasco sauce

large pinch cayenne pepper

salt and pepper

paprika, for dusting

sprigs of fresh dill, to garnish

method

To cook the eggs, put them in a pan, cover with cold water, and slowly bring to a boil. Immediately reduce the heat to very low, cover, and let simmer gently for 10 minutes. As soon as the eggs are cooked, drain, and put under cold running water to prevent a black ring from forming round the yolk. Gently tap the eggs to crack the shells and let stand until cold. When cold, remove the shells.

Using a stainless steel knife, halve the eggs lengthwise, then carefully remove the yolks. Put the yolks in a nylon strainer, set over a bowl, and rub through, then mash them with a wooden spoon or fork. If necessary, rinse the egg whites under cold water and dry very carefully.

Drain the pimientos on paper towels, then chop them finely, reserving a few strips. Finely chop the olives. Both ingredients need to be chopped very finely if you wish to pipe the mixture into the egg halves. Add the chopped pimientos and most of the chopped olives to the mashed egg yolks, reserving 16 larger pieces to garnish. Add the mayonnaise, mix well together, then add the Tabasco sauce, cayenne pepper, and salt and pepper to taste.

For a grand finale, put the egg yolk mixture into a pastry bag fitted with a $1/2$-inch/1-cm plain tip and pipe the mixture into the hollow egg whites. Alternatively, for a simpler finish, use a teaspoon to spoon the prepared filling into each egg half.

Arrange the eggs on a serving plate. Add a small strip of the reserved pimientos and a piece of olive to the top of each stuffed egg. Dust with a little paprika and garnish with dill sprigs.

eggs & cheese

ingredients

SERVES 6

6 hard-cooked eggs, cooled
and shelled

3 tbsp. grated manchego or
cheddar cheese

1–2 tbsp. mayonnaise

2 tbsp. snipped fresh chives

1 fresh red chili, seeded and
finely chopped

salt and pepper

lettuce leaves, to serve

method

Cut the eggs in half lengthwise and, using a teaspoon, carefully scoop out the yolks into a fine strainer, reserving the egg white halves. Rub the yolks through the strainer into a bowl and add the grated cheese, mayonnaise, chives, chili, and salt and pepper to taste.

Spoon the filling into the egg white halves.

Arrange a bed of lettuce on individual serving plates and top with the eggs. Cover and let chill until ready to serve.

flamenco eggs

ingredients

SERVES 4

4 tbsp. olive oil

1 onion, thinly sliced

2 garlic cloves, finely
    chopped

2 small red bell peppers,
    seeded and chopped

4 tomatoes, peeled, seeded,
    and chopped

1 tbsp. chopped fresh parsley

7 oz/200 g canned corn
    kernels, drained

4 eggs

salt and cayenne pepper

method

Preheat the oven to 350°F/180°C. Heat the olive oil in a large, heavy-bottom skillet. Add the onion and garlic and cook over low heat, stirring occasionally, for 5 minutes,or until softened. Add the red bell peppers and cook, stirring occasionally, for an additional 10 minutes. Stir in the tomatoes and parsley, season to taste with salt and cayenne and cook for an additional 5 minutes. Stir in the corn kernels and remove the skillet from the heat.

Divide the mixture between 4 individual ovenproof dishes. Make a hollow in the surface of each using the back of a spoon. Break an egg into each depression.

Bake in the preheated oven for 15–25 minutes, or until the eggs have set. Serve hot.

basque
scrambled eggs

ingredients

SERVES 4–6

3–4 tbsp. olive oil

1 large onion, finely chopped

1 large red bell pepper,
    seeded and chopped

1 large green bell pepper,
    seeded and chopped

2 large tomatoes, peeled,
    seeded, and chopped

2 oz/55 g chorizo sausage,
    sliced thinly, outer casing
    removed, if preferred

1¼ oz/35 g/generous ¼ stick
    butter

10 large eggs, lightly beaten

salt and pepper

4–6 thick slices country-style
    bread, toasted, to serve

method

Heat 2 tablespoons of olive oil in a large, heavy-bottom skillet over medium heat. Add the onion and bell peppers and cook for 5 minutes, or until the vegetables are softened but not browned. Add the tomatoes and heat through. Transfer to a heatproof plate and keep warm in a preheated low oven.

Add another tablespoon of oil to the skillet. Add the chorizo and cook for 30 seconds, just to warm through and flavor the oil. Add the sausage to the reserved vegetables.

Add a little extra olive oil, if necessary, to bring it back to 2 tablespoons. Add the butter and let melt. Season the eggs with salt and pepper, then add to the pan and scramble until cooked to the desired degree of firmness. Return the vegetables to the pan and stir through. Serve immediately with hot toast.

chorizo & quail's eggs

ingredients

MAKES 12

12 slices french bread, sliced
    on the diagonal, about
    1/4 inch/5 mm thick
1 1/2 oz/40 g cured,
    ready-to-eat chorizo,
    cut into 12 thin slices
olive oil
12 quail's eggs
mild paprika
salt and pepper
fresh flat-leaf parsley,
    to garnish

method

Preheat the broiler to high. Arrange the slices of bread on a baking sheet and broil until golden brown on both sides.

Cut or fold the chorizo slices to fit on the toasts, then reserve.

Heat a thin layer of olive oil in a large skillet over medium heat until a cube of bread sizzles—about 40 seconds. Break the eggs into the skillet and cook, spooning the fat over the yolks, until the whites are set and the yolks are cooked to your liking.

Remove the fried eggs from the skillet and drain on paper towels. Immediately transfer to the chorizo-topped toasts and dust with paprika. Season to taste with salt and pepper, then garnish with parsley and serve immediately.

deep-fried manchego cheese

ingredients

SERVES 6–8

7 oz/200 g manchego cheese

3 tbsp. all-purpose flour

salt and pepper

1 egg

1 tsp. water

3 oz/85 g/1¹/₂ cups fresh
    white or brown
    bread crumbs

corn oil, for deep-frying

method

Slice the cheese into triangular shapes about ²/₃ inch/ 2 cm thick or alternatively into cubes measuring about the same size. Put the flour in a plastic bag and season with salt and pepper to taste. Break the egg into a shallow dish and beat together with the water. Spread the bread crumbs onto a plate.

Toss the cheese pieces in the flour so that they are evenly coated, then dip the cheese in the egg mixture. Finally, dip the cheese in the bread crumbs so that the pieces are coated on all sides. Transfer to a large plate and store in the refrigerator until you are ready to serve them.

Just before serving, heat about 1 inch/2.5 cm of the corn oil in a large, heavy-bottom skillet or heat the oil in a deep-fryer to 350–375°F/180–190°C, or until a cube of bread browns in 30 seconds. Add the cheese pieces, in batches of about 4 or 5 pieces so that the temperature of the oil does not drop, and deep-fry for 1–2 minutes, turning once, until the cheese is just starting to melt and they are golden brown on all sides. Do make sure that the oil is hot enough, otherwise the coating on the cheese will take too long to become crisp and the cheese inside may ooze out.

Using a slotted spoon, remove the deep-fried cheese from the skillet or deep-fryer and drain well on paper towels. Serve the deep-fried cheese pieces hot, accompanied by toothpicks on which to spear them.

cheese puffs with fiery tomato salsa

ingredients

SERVES 8

2¹/₂ oz/70 g/scant ¹/₂ cup all-
 purpose flour
2 fl oz/50 ml/¹/₄ cup Spanish
 olive oil
5 fl oz/150 ml/²/₃ cup water
2 eggs, beaten
¹/₂ cup manchego, parmesan,
 cheddar, gouda, or
 gruyère cheese, finely
 grated
¹/₂ tsp. paprika
salt and pepper
corn oil, for deep-frying

fiery tomato salsa

2 tbsp. Spanish olive oil
1 small onion, finely chopped
1 garlic clove, crushed
splash of dry white wine
14 oz/400 g canned chopped
 tomatoes
1 tbsp. tomato paste
¹/₄–¹/₂ tsp. dried red pepper
 flakes
dash of tabasco sauce
pinch of sugar
salt and pepper

method

To make the salsa, heat the olive oil in a pan, add the onion and cook for 5 minutes, or until softened but not browned. Add the garlic and cook for an additional 30 seconds. Add the wine and let bubble, then add all the remaining salsa ingredients and let simmer, uncovered, for 10–15 minutes, or until a thick sauce is formed. Spoon into a serving bowl and set aside.

Meanwhile, prepare the cheese puffs. Sift the flour onto a plate or sheet of waxed paper. Put the olive oil and water in a pan and slowly bring to a boil. As soon as the water boils, remove the pan from the heat, and quickly tip in the flour all at once. Using a wooden spoon, beat the mixture well until it is smooth and leaves the sides of the pan.

Let the mixture cool for 1–2 minutes, then gradually add the eggs, beating hard after each addition and keeping the mixture stiff. Add the cheese and paprika, season to taste with salt and pepper, and mix well together.

To cook the cheese puffs, heat the corn oil in a deep-fryer to 350–375°F/180–190°C, or until a cube of bread browns in 30 seconds. Drop teaspoonfuls of the prepared mixture, in batches, into the hot oil and deep-fry for 2–3 minutes, turning once, or until golden and crispy. They should rise to the surface of the oil and puff up. Drain well on paper towels.

Serve the puffs piping hot, accompanied by the fiery salsa for dipping, and toothpicks to spear the puffs.

figs with bleu cheese

ingredients

SERVES 6

12 ripe figs

12 oz/350 g Spanish bleu
cheese, such as Picós,
crumbled

extra-virgin olive oil, to serve

caramelized almonds

3¹/2 oz/100 g/¹/2 cup
superfine sugar

4 oz/115 g whole almonds

butter, for greasing

method

First make the caramelized almonds. Place the sugar in
a pan over medium heat and stir until the sugar melts
and turns golden brown and bubbles. Do not stir once
the mixture begins to bubble. Remove the pan from the
heat, then add the almonds one at a time and quickly
turn with a fork until coated. If the caramel hardens, return
the pan to the heat. Transfer each almond to a lightly
greased baking sheet once it is coated. Let stand until
cool and firm.

To serve, slice the figs in half and arrange 4 halves on
individual serving plates. Coarsely chop the almonds by
hand. Place a mound of bleu cheese on each plate and
sprinkle with chopped almonds. Drizzle the figs very
lightly with the olive oil.

bean &
cabrales salad

ingredients

SERVES 4

5^1/$_2$ oz/150 g/scant 1 cup
    small dried great Northern
    beans, soaked for 4 hours
    or overnight

1 bay leaf

4 tbsp. olive oil

2 tbsp. sherry vinegar

2 tsp. clear honey

1 tsp. dijon mustard

salt and pepper

2 tbsp. toasted slivered
    almonds

7 oz/200 g cabrales or other
    bleu cheese, crumbled

method

Drain the beans and place in a large, heavy-bottom pan.
Pour in enough water to cover, then add the bay leaf and
bring to a boil. Boil for 1–1^1/$_2$ hours, or until tender. Drain,
then tip into a bowl and let cool slightly. Remove and
discard the bay leaf.

Meanwhile, make the dressing. Whisk the olive oil, vinegar,
honey, and mustard together in a bowl and season to taste
with salt and pepper. Pour the dressing over the beans
and toss lightly. Add the almonds and toss lightly again.
Let cool to room temperature.

Spoon the beans into individual serving bowls and scatter
over the cheese before serving.

cheese & shallots with herb dressing

ingredients

SERVES 6

1 tsp. sesame seeds
1/4 tsp. cumin seeds
4 tomatoes, seeded
    and diced
5 tbsp. olive oil
4 tbsp. lemon juice
2 tsp. chopped fresh thyme
1 tbsp. chopped fresh mint
4 shallots, finely chopped
1 lb 2 oz/500 g Idiazabal or
    other sheep's milk
    cheese, diced
salt and pepper

method

Dry-fry the sesame and cumin seeds in a small, heavy-bottom skillet, shaking the skillet frequently, until they begin to pop and give off their aroma. Remove the skillet from the heat and let cool.

Place the tomatoes in a bowl. To make the dressing, whisk the olive oil and lemon juice together in a separate bowl. Season to taste with salt and pepper, then add the thyme, mint, and shallots and mix well.

Place the cheese in another bowl. Pour half the dressing over the tomatoes and toss lightly. Cover with plastic wrap and let chill for 1 hour. Pour the remaining dressing over the cheese, then cover and chill for 1 hour.

To serve, divide the cheese mixture between 6 serving plates and sprinkle with half the toasted seeds. Top with the tomato mixture and sprinkle with the remaining toasted seeds.

roasted bell peppers with fiery cheese

ingredients

SERVES 6

1 red bell pepper, halved
and deseeded

1 orange bell pepper, halved
and deseeded

1 yellow bell pepper, halved
and deseeded

4 oz/115 g Afuega'l Pitu
cheese or other hot spiced
cheese, diced

1 tbsp. clear honey

1 tbsp. sherry vinegar

salt and pepper

method

Preheat the broiler to high. Place the bell peppers, skin-side up, in a single layer on a baking sheet. Cook under the hot broiler for 8–10 minutes, or until the skins have blistered and blackened. Using tongs, transfer to a plastic bag. Tie the top and let cool.

When the bell peppers are cool enough to handle, peel off the skin with your fingers or a knife and discard it. Place on a serving plate and sprinkle over the cheese.

Whisk the honey and vinegar together in a bowl and season to taste with salt and pepper. Pour the dressing over the bell peppers, then cover and let chill until required.

burgos with sherry vinegar

ingredients

SERVES 4

14 oz/400 g Burgos cheese

1–2 tbsp. clear honey

3 tbsp. sherry vinegar

carrot sticks

chilled sherry, to serve

method

Place the cheese in a bowl and beat until smooth, then beat in 1 tablespoon of the honey and $1^1/_2$ tablespoons of the vinegar.

Taste and adjust the sweetness to your liking by adding more honey or more vinegar as required.

Divide between 4 small serving bowls, then cover and let chill until required. Serve with carrot sticks and chilled sherry.

cheese & olive empanadillas

ingredients

MAKES 26

3 oz/85 g firm or soft cheese

3 oz/85 g/ 1/2 cup pitted green
olives

2 oz/55 g/1/4 cup sundried
tomatoes in oil, drained

13/4 oz/50 g canned
anchovies, drained

pepper

2 tbsp. sundried tomato paste

all-purpose flour, for dusting

1 lb 2 oz/500 g ready-made
puff pastry, thawed if frozen

beaten egg, to glaze

fresh flat-leaf parsley sprigs,
to garnish

method

Preheat the oven to 400°F/200°C. Cut the cheese into small dice measuring about 1/4 inch/5 mm. Chop the olives, sundried tomatoes, and anchovies into pieces about the same size as the cheese. Put all the chopped ingredients in a bowl, season with pepper to taste, and gently mix together. Stir in the sundried tomato paste.

On a lightly floured counter, thinly roll out the puff pastry. Using a plain, round 31/4-inch/8-cm cutter, cut into 18 circles. Gently pile the trimmings together, roll out again, then cut out an additional 8 circles. Using a teaspoon, put a little of the prepared filling equally in the center of each of the pastry circles.

Dampen the edges of the pastry with a little water, then bring up the sides to completely cover the filling and pinch the edges together with your fingers to seal them. With the tip of a sharp knife, make a small slit in the top of each pastry. You can store the pastries in the refrigerator at this stage until you are ready to bake them.

Place the pastries onto dampened baking sheets and brush each with a little beaten egg to glaze. Bake in the oven for 10–15 minutes, or until golden brown, crisp and well risen. Serve the empanadillas piping hot, warm, or cold, garnished with parsley sprigs.